The Assassination File

Books by Brian Bailey

HANGMEN OF ENGLAND
THE ASSASSINATION FILE

THE
ASSASSINATION
FILE

Brian Bailey

W H ALLEN

First published in Great Britain in 1991 by
W. H. Allen
26 Grand Union Centre
338 Ladbroke Grove
London W10 5AH

Copyright © Brian Bailey 1991

British Library Cataloguing in Publication data
Bailey, Brian J. (Brian John) 1934–
    The assassination file.
    1. Murder, history
    I. Title
    364.1524

    ISBN 1 85227 203 1

Set in 11/12pt Times by Phoenix Photosetting, Chatham, Kent
Printed and bound in Great Britain by
Mackays of Chatham PLC, Chatham, Kent

Contents

Illustrations

(All pictures, unless otherwise indicated, are reproduced courtesy of the Mansell Collection.)

between pp. 84 and 85

Introduction: What's in a Name?

'Assassination,' Disraeli said, 'has never changed the history of the world.' And in terms of the broad sweep of history, he was undoubtedly right. Assassination has often accompanied world-shattering events, such as the French Revolution, but has been incidental to them, although it has sometimes achieved short-term results, for better or worse. What is more important, and highly regrettable, is that it has become ever more common. Edward Hyams reckoned that the half-century between 1865 and 1914 was what he called the 'golden age' of assassination. Notwithstanding his dubious choice of words, Hyams was wrong. The years after 1914 have seen many more.

Before embarking on the long and shocking history of what we call assassination, however, I would like to consider the word itself. It did not exist in the ancient world. Although it appears in the Revised Version of the Bible (Acts 21:38), it is merely a poor translation of the Greek *sikarioi*, from the word for 'dagger'. (It is rendered as 'murderers' in the Authorised Version.) The Latin *sicarii* were members of a Roman secret society who committed sudden murders of their enemies, and whose practices were imitated by Jews of the political party of Zealots in Palestine in the period of the Roman Republic.

The word 'assassin' seems to be a medieval Latin version of the Arabic *hassasin*, the plural of *hassas*, meaning 'hashish-eater'. The name was originally given to a sect of Shi'ite Muslim fanatics founded at the time of the Crusades by Hassan ibn-al-Sabbah, known as the 'Old Man of the Mountain' because he led a revolt against the Seljuks from his mountain stronghold in Lebanon. One of the sect's practices was to carry out the secret elimination of its enemies, like the ancient *sicarii*, and Hassan's hit-men, or *fedayeen*, were reputed to be doped with hashish when they went forth on their murderous missions. Hence the use of the term *hassasin*, strictly within its original meaning. But that was in the Middle Ages, and the sect's power ended in the thirteenth century when 12,000 of its members were massacred by Mongol invaders under their warlord Hulagu, grandson of Genghis Khan. What useful purpose, then, does a westernised version of the word serve as used today?

It is one of those foreign words which the English language so readily absorbs and which we soon take very much for granted. And not only the English. Edward Gibbon, referring to the extirpation of the Assassins as 'a service to mankind', wrote that not a vestige of them is left, 'except the word *assassin*, which, in the most odious sense, has been adopted in the languages of Europe'.

The most comprehensive study of assassination I am aware of is the report to the National Commission on the Causes and Prevention of Violence set up by President Lyndon Johnson in 1968, following the death of Senator Robert Kennedy. But the report starts off on a negative note: its inability to define exactly what the word 'assassination' means. Several other books also begin with very woolly definitions of the word.

It seems to me that a foreign word with no precise meaning has no place in the English language. Everyone knows what 'murder' means, and I believe that by calling murder 'assassination' we lend the act overtones of dignity, and even virtue, to which it has no entitlement, and this is not merely unnecessary but positively unhelpful and probably dangerous. The use of the word by modern and relatively civilised societies with well developed languages is surely an example of that kind of euphemism which Simon Hoggart has called 'Grand Guignol vocabulary'.

Other writers, extending the use of the word beyond its dictionary definition as the killing of a political or religious leader, have employed it to describe the (alleged) killing of Mozart, that of the poet Lorca, the outlaw Jesse James, and the pop idol John Lennon, among others. Queen Joanna I of Naples had her husband Andrew of Hungary killed in the fourteenth century because she found him personally repellent, and his death has been described as assassination. If we accept this, then almost *any* murder can be called assassination, and one word or the other might as well be made redundant. Even the discharge of an empty pistol at Queen Victoria has frequently been included among stories of 'attempted assassinations'. Such stretching of the word's usage shows exactly where its danger lies. It glamorises the act of murder or attempted murder, and there is no doubt that the glamour of it is attractive to many – perhaps most – of the disturbed individuals who have set out to kill 'very important persons' prompted only by their own psychological frustrations.

Granted that we wish to distinguish the killing of a head of state for political reasons from the sordid and insignificant murders of everyday life in the backstreets of history, we have words enough to choose from. The killing of a king is regicide; the killing of a tyrant, tyrannicide; that of a sacred person, parricide. All of them are also homicide.

Assassination cannot be defined simply as murder in public, for it is often carried out in great secrecy; nor can I accept the distinction made by Colin Wilson that a murderer is a killer with a guilty secret, whereas an assassin proclaims his public act. The exhibitionist 'assassin' who craves attention is often simply a demented murderer, and his irrational act the result of mental instability rather than considered judgement. Even if an individual acts for political reasons, that does not qualify his act as assassination: in my view, assassination must be the result of a consensus of opinion.

I would suggest, since it is unlikely the word 'assassination' will ever be abandoned, that it should be confined to the murder of an elite personage by, or at the behest of, a group which believes itself, rightly or wrongly, to be acting in the best interests of the people. But even this definition has its problems, for not all eminent persons killed during military *coups d'état* can be called assassination victims. It is also doubtful whether victims of terrorist raids or gangland killings can be regarded as assassinees, even if their deaths were deliberately planned. Can we refer to the death, for instance, of President Salvador Allende of Chile, who was apparently shot in a gun battle during a military coup in 1973, as assassination? When the overthrow of the government is the object of the exercise, rather than the elimination of a key individual, assassination is not the priority. Certainly the killing of any eminent person by an individual motivated by a private grudge or dream of glory is plain murder, and if that takes the glamour out of many so-called assassinations so much the better.

The killing of Julius Caesar was assassination. That of John F. Kennedy, if the Warren Commission's report is to be believed, was murder. However, it is not always clear which was which, and in this book I range freely over some incidents which are commonly referred to as assassinations, though not always agreeing with the definition myself.

Having made my point here, I leave the reader to judge for himself how often in history the act of violence, and the word used to describe it, have been necessary. Because of space limitations, I have confined my choice of subjects mainly, though not exclusively, to heads of state and political leaders, some good, others unquestionably evil. But what they all had in common was that they assumed power over other people's lives, and paid for it in the end when, as was inevitable, they failed to please all of the people all of the time.

1

The King Must Die

The Cult of Osiris in ancient Egypt embraced a proposition
which has had a profound currency, conscious or otherwise,
throughout the subsequent history of the world, and which
seems itself to have originated in beliefs going far back into
prehistory. It held that the wellbeing of a tribe or a people
derived from the sacred or divine person of its king. The
king's power was essentially life-enhancing, and his strength
vital for the survival of his people. It ensured the fertility and
health of his subjects, their crops and their livestock. It followed, therefore, that when the king grew old or feeble the
tribe was threatened. The solution to this problem was
obvious. When a king began to show signs of weakness or
senility, he had to be sacrificed, and replaced by a young and
vigorous successor.

Although there is no proof that the pharaohs of the Old
Kingdom of Egypt were ever actually killed, anthropologists
have made much of the idea of the scapegoat. Sir James
Frazer cited the ritual killing of kings in many parts of Africa,
the Middle East and India, and in some places the idea
remained potent up to the nineteenth century, albeit largely
symbolically.

We do know of at least two historical conspiracies against
Egyptian pharaohs and one suspicious death. In the Middle
Kingdom the king, Amonemhat I, wrote an account of a plot
against himself for the benefit and warning of his son and
successor: '. . . the men who came against me,' he wrote,
'with their daggers sharp and keen, were the men whom I had
trusted and enriched . . . A serpent of the desert they had
called me in their plots; as a serpent of the desert I was ready
for the fray. Weapons gleamed and flashed around me, but I
struck the traitors down.'

It is possible that the pharaoh Tutankhamun was assassinated. The boy-king came to the Egyptian throne in 1361 BC, at the age of about eight, in a period of religious and political instability in the kingdom, and was dead by 1352 BC, though still only a youth, to be succeeded by his chief minister Ay. Examination of the mummified body of Tutankhamun, discovered by Howard Carter in 1922, produced no evidence of the cause of his early death. He left a young widow but no offspring, and the widowed queen wrote a letter to the King of the Hittites asking him to send her one of his sons as a husband to secure the succession. But the young prince was murdered on his journey, by agents of Ay, and Tutankhamun's widow then disappears from history. Possibly Tutankhamun's surprisingly early death was the result of a plot provoked by the religious heresy of his father-in-law, Akhenaton, which Tutankhamun first embraced and then rejected. We shall never know.

Ramses III, who died in 1116 BC, was a victim of a conspiracy in his own harem. Ramses reigned over Egypt for 32 years, and was a mighty warrior. But one of his wives, Tyi, instigated a plot to replace the ageing king with her son, and was joined by other women and some of the household servants. They first tried to kill the pharaoh by magic, using wax images, but when the assassination by remote control failed to work they undertook a more direct attack on his person. Ramses survived long enough to identify twelve conspirators who were sentenced to death, and others who had their ears and noses cut off before being imprisoned, but he died shortly afterwards. The death of Ramses can certainly be seen as a sacrificial killing – in Freudian terms, it was a classic case of the rivalry between father and son.

The life of a sovereign is only valuable, Sir James Frazer wrote, 'so long as he discharges the duties of his position by ordering the course of nature for his people's benefit. So soon as he fails to do so, the care, the devotion, the religious homage which they had hitherto lavished on him cease and are changed into hatred and contempt; he is dismissed ignominiously, and may be thankful if he escapes with his life. Worshipped as a god one day, he is killed as a criminal the next . . . If their king is their god, he is or should be also their preserver; and if he will not preserve them, he must make room for another who will.'

The Shilluk people of Sudan took it as a sure sign of their king's dangerous weakness if he could no longer satisfy the sexual demands of his many wives; and the principle was carried to its logical extreme by a tribe in the Congo which evidently put a new king to death on the night after his coronation. Thus the tribe ensured that it never suffered the ill-effects resulting from an ailing king. 'The mystic kings of Fire and Water in Cambodia,' Frazer tells us, 'are not allowed to die a natural death. Hence when one of them is seriously ill and the elders think that he cannot recover, they stab him to death.' The prehistoric kings of Babylon, according to some authorities, were allowed to reign for only one year, at the end of which they were ritually sacrificed.

The idea is common enough in mythology, most notably, perhaps, in the unwitting murder by Oedipus of his father, King Laius of Thebes, whom he succeeded. In Crete, the annual tribute of Athenian youths and maidens to King Minos, who fed them to the Minotaur, was probably a variation on the common notion of a surrogate king being sacrificed in a ritual of rebirth or renewal. The Norse god Odin, mythical ancestor of the kings of Sweden, demanded from one of them the sacrifice of a son every ninth year – the maximum period of tenure of the throne, at which point the king would be put to death himself unless he produced the substitute required by the god. The king lived to a ripe and feeble old age by sacrificing nine of his ten sons in this way at Uppsala, before dying himself.

Often merely taking the form of a ceremony of rejuvenation every few years, the sacrifice of a king – the real or symbolic death of one man for the sake of the people – gained wide currency. The idea was most famously exploited by Christianity which received it from the Jews. When the Romans executed Jesus of Nazareth, 'King of the Jews', for sedition, his death was readily elevated by his followers into an act of self-sacrifice to 'save the world'. When Caiaphas had said, '. . . consider that it is expedient of us, that one man should die for the people, and that the whole nation perish not,' (John 11:50), the High Priest had a rather narrower political end in mind than Christians subsequently accorded to Jesus, but still the general principle was the same. Christianity also perpetuated these ideas in its ritual of the Eucharist, symbolically eating the body and drinking the blood of the dead king in order to consume his strength and virtue.

Political assassination, too, is common enough in the biblical accounts of the kings of Israel and Judah. For instance: 'In the twenty and seventh year of Asa king of Judah did Zimri reign seven days in Tirzah. And the people were encamped against Gibbethon, which belonged to the Philistines. And the people that were encamped heard say, Zimri hath conspired, and hath also slain the king . . .' (I Kings 16:15–16). And again: 'In the fiftieth year of Azariah king of Judah Pekahiah the son of Menahem began to reign over Israel in Samaria, and reigned two years. And he did that which was evil in the sight of the Lord: he departed not from the sins of Jeroboam the son of Nebat, who made Israel to sin. But Pekah the son of Remaliah, a captain of his, conspired against him, and smote him in Samaria, in the palace of the king's house, with Argob and Arieh, and with him fifty men of the Gileadites: and he killed him, and reigned in his room.' (II Kings 15:23–25). These events are reckoned to have occurred about 907 and 750 BC respectively.

Perhaps the best known assassination of the Old Testament, however, is that of Sennacherib, King of Assyria, in 681 BC. The story is told in both Chronicles and Isaiah, how Sennacherib invaded Judah but was finally defeated, partly by the intervention of a guardian angel and partly by the ingenuity of Hezekiah, King of Judah, who blocked or diverted all the springs so that Sennacherib's army, encamped outside the very gates of Jerusalem, had no water. And when Sennacherib went home to Ninevah in shame, having lost more than 5000 men, 'it came to pass, as he was worshipping in the house of Nisroch his god, that Adrammelech and Sharezer his sons smote him with the sword; and they escaped into the land of Armenia: and Esar-haddon his son reigned in his stead.' Never was there a plainer example of a ritual sacrifice!

One of the more significant so-called assassinations of the ancient Greek world was that of Hipparchus in 514 BC. His killing at the hands of the aristocrats Harmodius and

Aristogiton was interpreted by later Athenians as a noble act to rid the people of a tyrant. Hipparchus had indeed inherited the tyranny of his father Pisistratus, along with his elder brother Hippias, but his killing was a purely personal matter. The two young aristocrats were lovers, and Hipparchus had made advances to one of them which had been rejected. They feared the possible consequences from the tyrannical family, and at first planned to kill Hippias, but then fell upon Hipparchus instead. It was simple homicide, but became glamorised in the course of time as a sacrifice for the sake of liberty.

Among the early historical examples of regicide for which we now use the word assassination was the murder of Philip of Macedon in 336 BC. Philip had reigned for 23 years, a military leader of genius and an astute statesman, who unified the Greek states. It was whilst the king was celebrating the marriage of his daughter that Pausanias, a youth of distinguished family and a member of the royal bodyguard, stabbed the one-eyed monarch to death. The murderer was captured immediately as he was trying to make his escape on waiting horses. He thus had accomplices, and two brothers were convicted and executed – probably by stoning – for complicity in the murder. Pausanias himself was probably clamped to a stake and starved to death.

The precise motive for the murder is not known. It may have been a purely personal matter, some saying that Philip had ignored a complaint which the young man, who had been his lover, had made to him; or that the king's rejected wife Olympias put Pausanias up to it. In either of these cases the crime was simple murder. But Philip had been preparing for a war against Persia, and the killing may have been arranged by Persian agents or on behalf of those within Greece opposed to his dangerous ambitions, for, as Demosthenes had said in his famous *Second Oration against Philip*, 'ambition is his great passion, universal empire the sole object of his views; not peace, not tranquillity, not any just purpose'. If Philip's death *was* a political assassination, it was, if anything, counter-productive, for the king was immediately succeeded by his son, and his son was Alexander the Great!

Some have even suspected that Alexander himself may have had a hand in the murder. He had been at odds with his father over Philip's repudiation of his mother. But there is no evidence for such an interpretation, and perhaps the most likely explanation of the killing is that Pausanias had a personal grudge against the king, as Aristotle believed. Alexander himself seems to have thought the Persians responsible. Whether the killing was murder or assassination, it was certainly regicide, and it is not difficult to see the death of Philip of Macedon as a ritual sacrifice, involving the displacement of an old king by a young god. The killing five years later of Darius III of Persia can also be seen in this light.

Darius had spent most of his brief reign in trying to defend the Persian empire against Alexander but he was an incompetent commander. He had been humiliated by the Macedonian conqueror, and became the victim of a conspiracy headed by the satrap Bessus, who was proclaimed king by his troops. Darius was given a royal funeral by Alexander, but it was almost a year before Bessus was captured. He was flogged, his nose and ears were cut off, and then he was executed for the crime of regicide. Why should Alexander so punish the killer of his enemy? Because he believed in the divinity of kings, and it was important to discourage anyone from contemplating the killing of a king. Alexander believed himself to be descended from Zeus with a divine mission, and he respected the person of the king of Persia. It is clear that if Darius had fallen into Alexander's hands, he would not have been killed, and indeed would have remained in authority over Persia within Alexander's empire.

There was a conspiracy to assassinate Alexander himself later, hatched among his pages – young sons of noblemen, who were being trained as royal servants and acted as bodyguards. But the plot was discovered before any blow was struck, and the youthful conspirators were, in all likelihood, stoned to death.

After Alexander's death from fever in 323 BC, his second wife, the Bactrian princess Roxane, gave birth to his son and heir, and named him Alexander, but both mother and son were murdered in 311 BC as a result of the collapse of the empire and the ensuing rivalry of aspiring rulers. Taking refuge in Europe, Roxane and Alexander were murdered by order of the general Cassander, who had taken possession of

Macedonia. The boy was guilty of no crime save being his father's son, but Roxane was not so innocent. She had been responsible for the murder of another of Alexander's wives, Statira, the daughter of Darius III, by poisoning. In 309 BC Alexander's first wife and child, Barsine and her son Heracles, were likewise eliminated from any contest for the fruits of Alexander's empire.

The Seleucid kings of Syria were brought down by assassination with such regularity that it hints at ritual sacrifice. The founder of that dynasty, Seleucus I, was murdered in 280 BC by his rival Ptolemy, King of Egypt, as he was about to seize the throne of Macedonia in the wars resulting from the rush to carve up Alexander's empire. Seleucus III and V also fell victim to assassination, the former by his own troops and the latter at the instigation of his mother, Cleopatra, who was outraged by his assumption of the crown on the death of his father, Demetrius.

The murder of the Carthaginian leader Hasdrubal in 221 BC has been described frequently as assassination, but he was killed by a slave seeking vengeance for the execution of his father, and this was clearly a case of simple murder.

The Jewish patriot Simon Maccabeus *was* a victim of assassination, however, in 135 BC. The younger brother of the hero Judas Maccabeus, he succeeded his brother Jonathan as military leader and high priest of the Jewish people, for whom he won the support of Rome and complete independence from Syria. But his son-in-law Ptolemy, governor of Jericho, coveted the leadership of the country for himself, and he entertained Simon at a great banquet. 'When Simon and his sons had drunk largely,' as the Apocrypha tells the story, 'Ptolemee [sic] and his men rose up, and took their weapons, and came upon Simon into the banqueting place, and slew him, and his two sons, and certain of his servants. In which doing he committed a great treachery, and recompensed evil for good.' (1 Maccabees 16:16–17). The murder did Ptolemy no good whatever. Simon's third son John Hyrcanus, having been forewarned of Ptolemy's intention of killing him also, took the necessary action and succeeded his father, becoming founder of the Jewish monarchy. Hyrcanus died in 104 BC, about two years before the birth of one whose name was to go down in history as a major victim of party politics functioning as a blood sport.

Gaius Julius Caesar, reputedly plucked from his mother's womb by a surgical method which has ever since borne his name, was the son of patrician parents with important connections that put him on the first rungs of the ladder to fame and fortune in the Roman republic. His early manhood was a mixture of scandalous sexual alliances and dangerous political ones. He was suspected of having a homosexual relationship with King Nicomodes III of Bithynia, and was called 'Queen of Bithynia' behind his back. He also seduced several women of noble birth and had numerous mistresses, and was once referred to in public as 'every woman's husband and every man's wife'.

But he married Cornelia, daughter of Cinna, leader of the popular party in Rome, and won the favour of Marius, the people's champion and chief opponent of Sulla, the dictator and leader of the aristocratic party. Caesar thus incurred Sulla's enmity, and had to go into hiding for a time. After Sulla's victory in the ensuing civil war, the young Julius Caesar's life was in real danger, and it was spared only on account of special pleading by his aristocratic relations and because he was not seen as a serious political threat to anyone – his preoccupations in life in his early twenties were sex and luxury. Even after he had made his way to the centre of Roman politics, Cicero, the orator and implacable enemy of dictatorships, said that he could not imagine the idea of subverting the Roman state ever entering the head of this man.

After Sulla's death in 78 BC, however, Caesar's rise to eminence began. His ambitions for power at home brought him to the fore in Roman politics, and his military campaigns abroad brought him wealth and public acclamation. Soon his only rivals as leaders of the republic were the great soldier Pompey, who had once opposed Marius and been honoured by Sulla with the title Pompeius Magnus but who now identified himself with the popular party, and Crassus, the general who had ruthlessly suppressed the revolt led by Spartacus and whose immense wealth had supported some of Caesar's ventures. Julius Caesar formed a coalition with his two fellow generals, which was further cemented by the marriage of Pompey to Caesar's daughter. The triumvirate of the popular or democratic party replaced the oligarchic government of the republican or conservative party with its class privileges and backward-looking ideals.

Caesar spent the next nine years in military conquest, earning the adulation and loyalty of his troops by his bravery and brilliant leadership, and bringing large parts of Europe under the rule of Rome. But during his absence, the triumvirate broke down. Crassus was killed during an ill-fated invasion of Mesopotamia, and Pompey's wife Julia died young. Though Pompey was Caesar's son-in-law, he was the senior of the two by four or five years, and was jealous of the younger man's ever-increasing success and popularity. While Caesar was preoccupied in Gaul, Pompey began to pass laws in the senate which favoured his own advancement at Caesar's expense, and in due course he was elected sole consul. The break was now complete, and a confrontation between them inevitable.

Pompey returned to the bosom of his spiritual host, the aristocratic party. Senators had been persuaded that Caesar intended to use his military might to sack Rome and establish himself as dictator. He was called upon to renounce his military commands and return to Rome as a private citizen. But in January 49 BC Caesar crossed the Rubicon with his troops in a show of strength. Technically it was an act of treason, and Pompey now had to defend the republic against him. Pompey withdrew to raise an army in the east, and panic-stricken senators fled from Rome. But Caesar first diverted his army to Spain, winning over Pompey's army of occupation there, and only then returned to Rome, restoring order and dispelling all notions of destructive intentions on his part. Then he set off for Greece to settle matters with Pompey, emerging triumphant from the decisive encounter at Pharsalus. Pompey fled to Alexandria and there, in 48 BC, he was stabbed to death by a former centurion, Septimus, acting on behalf of Ptolemy, King of Egypt, and his head was presented to his father-in-law when Caesar arrived in pursuit. Caesar lingered in Egypt and added Cleopatra to his

9

collection of lovers whilst his sycophantic deputy Mark Antony looked after Rome – and himself – in Caesar's absence.

Julius Caesar was now sole ruler of the Roman republic, and he returned to the city in triumph for a short time before setting off again to mop up all remaining opposition to his dictatorship in the provinces. Now in his mid-fifties, Caesar had the Roman world at his feet, and he was king in all but name. He set out to make practical improvements and social reforms and carry out public works for the benefit of the people. His dictatorship was benevolent, and he was not vindictive, but perhaps his military and political brilliance led him into a misjudged self-confidence in not only *forgiving* former enemies, such as Pompey's supporters, the generals Cassius and Brutus, but raising them again to positions of power. And it was he who restored the statues of Sulla and Pompey which had been smashed by the mob.

By overthrowing Roman traditions in his reorganisation of the senate, by swallowing the flattery of his sycophants, and by indulging his own extravagant self-esteem, he alienated conservatives who saw this autocracy leading the republic back to the monarchy that had been rejected for constitutional government 500 years earlier. He offended the senate by failing to observe the customary courtesy of rising to greet the senators as they came before him. In his reform of the calendar, he allowed the seventh month to be named July in his honour. He wore the laurel wreath and the military title *Imperator*. He permitted his puppets to erect a statue of him alongside those of the ancient kings of Rome, and to have a gilt throne placed in the senate for him. He allowed them to call him Jupiter Julius in a ritual of farcical idolisation. He reputedly entertained ideas of further conquest in the east; of rivalling Alexander the Great; of establishing Alexandria as the capital of a Roman empire with Cleopatra as his consort. He was an ageing, vain and epileptic demagogue, who, by shrewdly refusing the crown when it was offered to him, had the mob weeping in admiration of the great man's modesty and humility.

The conspiracy against him took shape quickly in the hands of Cassius. Scornful of superstition, Caesar ignored the warnings of soothsayers to beware the Ides of March, as well as the pleadings of his wife, and went to a meeting of the senate on 15 March 44 BC. There he was done to death at the base of Pompey's statue, as if it were a sacrificial altar, and pulled his toga over his face as his body received the flashing blades of his assassins' daggers and sank to the floor in a pool of blood.

According to Suetonius, the conspirators numbered more than 60 but how many took part in the actual killing is not clear. There were 23 stab wounds in the corpse. It was said that Caesar anticipated and even welcomed the sudden manner of his end, hating the idea of a lingering death. 'Let it come suddenly and unexpectedly,' he had said.

The murder of Julius Caesar remains probably the most famous in the history of the world, the prototype of political assassination. It was one of the few such killings on record that, because of its nature, *demands* some name other than simple murder. It was hardly regicide, because Caesar was not a king. It was scarcely tyrannicide, because although the assassins claimed to have carried out the deed on behalf of liberty, for the sake of Rome's future, Caesar's rule was not oppressive or intolerable, and the 'liberty' they spoke of was really the freedom of the privileged minority. Some might have called it parricide – the killing of a divine being. But the general reaction to the news was not, at first, one of outrage. The senate did not declare the killing an act of treason, and no action was taken against the conspirators, except by the fickle mob whose emotions were aroused later by the public reading of Caesar's will.

The justice of the killing is still debated. Many have seen Brutus and Cassius as champions of liberty; others as history's worst traitors, whom Dante consigned to the uttermost depths of the *Inferno* along with Judas Iscariot. But there is no arguing about the outcome of their action. The short-term result was civil war. If the assassins had killed Mark Antony too, this might have been avoided, but Brutus was against killing anyone but Caesar. 'Let's be sacrificers, but not butchers,' as Shakespeare makes him say. The long-term result, however, was precisely what the killing had been intended to prevent. Instead of kings, Rome got emperors.

Caesar's murderers had mistaken the man for the movement, and thought that by killing the individual they would kill the idea he represented. It was to be a common error of assassins through the centuries. After the *Pax Romana* under Caesar's heir Octavius – the emperor Augustus – Rome succumbed to greater tyranny, bloodshed, vice and corruption than ever before.

Meanwhile, in 43 BC, Antipater, whom Caesar himself had appointed procurator of Judaea, had been assassinated. Antipater, an Edomite, wrested power from Hyrcanus II, the last of the Maccabee rulers, and finding favour with Rome, especially after he had supported Caesar in his campaign against Pompey in Egypt, was rewarded in 47 BC with Roman citizenship as well as the procuratorship. But Antipater fell into the error of nepotism, making one of his sons governor of Jerusalem and another governor of Galilee. This was seen by patriotic Jews as a blatant attempt to set up an Edomite dynasty over them, and Antipater was poisoned, one year after Caesar's death.

His son Herod, the governor of Galilee, then won the confidence of Mark Antony and Octavius and was made king of Judaea, becoming known to history as Herod the Great, but his appalling tyranny made him notorious as a man of 'great barbarity towards all men equally', as Josephus describes him. Among the many victims of his cruelty, which may be classed as domestic murder, assassination or execution, were his two sons, Alexander and Aristobulus, by one of his ten wives, Mariamne. Later he married another woman also named Mariamne, and he was persuaded in due course that she and her mother Alexandra, a Maccabee widow who was in league with Cleopatra, were plotting against him, so he had them killed, too. Then in 4 BC he had his eldest son Antipater, by his first wife Doris, killed only five days before his own miserable end from plague in Jericho when, as the New Testament describes it, 'the angel of the Lord smote him . . . and he was eaten of worms, and gave up the ghost,' (Acts 12:23). It was after the death of Herod the Great's grandson Agrippa I that the *sicarii* emerged in the political chaos of Palestine.

Assassination became commonplace in the lurid politics of the early Roman empire. The killing of emperors usually had political motives, though the victims would have considered themselves divine sacrificial victims, especially the first to die by treachery – Caligula. The much-debated question whether Caligula was insane or not hardly matters here. Probably his reputation has suffered at the hands of ancient historians, much as Richard III's has at the hands of the Tudors. But the epileptic emperor clearly became an unspeakable tyrant, and in AD 41 he was slaughtered by the officers of the Praetorian Guard, the imperial bodyguard organised by Augustus and increased in numbers by Caligula himself. His extreme provocation of the Roman people, whom he once publicly wished had 'only one neck', made his murder the first historical example of regicide which we can say unequivocally was wholly justified. He caused the deaths of many for no other end than his personal whims, and if he was not sacrificed in order to be replaced by a younger and more vigorous emperor (he was only 29 and was succeeded by his uncle, Claudius), he was certainly killed for the sake of the people in another sense, and rightly so. His murder was the culmination of several plots against his life. According to Suetonius, so terrified were the people of Caligula that many were hesitant to accept reports of his death, thinking it a trick of the emperor to find out what they thought of him, and woe betide them if they did not think well!

Some say that Claudius was murdered, by his fourth wife Agrippina, who fed him poisonous mushrooms in order to secure the succession of her son Nero to the imperial purple, but there is no proof of that. Nero, however, did have Agrippina, his mother, murdered, on the grounds that *she* was plotting against *him*! After a failed attempt to drown her at sea, naval officers first hit her on the head with a truncheon, then ran her through with their swords, Agrippina directing them – according to Tacitus – to strike at her womb. From that womb by her marriage to Claudius had issued the epileptic Britannicus, whom Nero had also had murdered, by poison, when the boy was but fourteen years old. As an imperial prince, Britannicus had all his food and drink tasted, but his assassins gave him a harmless drink which was deliberately made too hot, and when the anticipated complaint came, they cooled it down by pouring in cold water to which poison had been added. After the killing of Agrippina, the philosopher Seneca, who owed his position to Agrippina, made a shameful speech in the senate attempting to justify the act, which was not only assassination but matricide, and he was so successful that the senate actually congratulated Nero for killing his mother.

The next *definite* imperial victim of assassination after Caligula was Galba. He succeeded Nero, but, having bought the allegiance of the army with bribes, he failed to make good his promises, and was murdered in a street of Rome by soldiers in a *coup d'état*, having reigned only six months. He is said to have challenged his murderers, as they attacked him, 'Strike, if it be for the good of Rome!' His head was paraded round on the end of a spear by his assassins. Vitellius, who ruled soon after Galba for only a few months in AD 69, was also murdered by his soldiers in an empire whose throne was now up for grabs and whose constitution seemed to be based on the survival of the fittest.

The unpopular emperor Domitian was stabbed to death in his bedroom in AD 96 by a group of conspirators in a palace revolution. His cruelty and tyranny were legendary, and there had been other plots to overthrow him. All emperors' lives were wretched, he had said, because it was only when they were actually murdered that people were convinced that the conspiracies they feared were real ones.

Commodus was justified in that fear. The son of the wise and learned emperor Marcus Aurelius, he was as brutish as his father was cultured, and one of the few criticisms levelled against Marcus Aurelius was that, as Gibbon put it, he 'sacrificed the happiness of millions to a fond partiality for a worthless boy'. The succession of Marcus's son brought an immediate end to the age of the Antonines, who had given Rome a century of good government. Commodus was strangled by a professional wrestler in AD 192, at the instigation of the prefect of the Praetorian Guard and other members of his household, and was replaced by an emperor carefully chosen to justify the assassination by the contrast between his prudence and integrity and the cruelty and debauchery of his predecessor. But Pertinax's policy of reform for the public good also provoked the hostility of the Praetorian Guard, which had become used to having things its own way, and he had reigned hardly three months when he, too, was cut down at the gates of the imperial palace and his head paraded through the streets on the point of a lance. His death was hardly in the public interest. The military faction responsible for it put the Roman empire up for auction.

The bloody catalogue of regicide continued when Getsa was cut down by his elder brother Caracella and his officers in AD 211, in their mother's apartment, and she was wounded in trying to protect one of her sons from the other. Caracella was himself stabbed to death in AD 217 at the instigation of a Praetorian prefect, Macrinus. Then Alexander Severus was murdered in his bed by his own troops in AD 235. He had been a tolerant and benevolent emperor.

Several later emperors were murdered, too, mostly in army revolts arising from some grudge or other that officers had against the presiding emperors. One of the more interesting cases was that of Julius Nepos, son-in-law of the Byzantine emperor Leo I. Nepos ruled the western empire from June AD 474 to August 475, but was then forced by invasion to take refuge in his principality of Dalmatia. The usurper, however, was soon deposed by another rival, the German Odoacer, who proclaimed himself King of Italy instead of Roman emperor. He and Nepos then both pressed their claims for recognition on the new eastern emperor Zeno (also Leo's son-in-law). Zeno decided in favour of Odoacer's position, but urged him to afford proper recognition to Nepos, who thus recovered his title of emperor in the west alongside the ruler of the new kingdom but did not resume his place in Rome. In May AD 480, Nepos was murdered in his house in Dalmatia by two of his servants. The probable instigator was the former emperor Glycerius, who had been overthrown by Nepos and palmed off with the bishopric of Salonae, subsequently becoming Archbishop of Milan. The barbarian King of Italy, Odoacer, then marched on Dalmatia ostensibly to avenge the assassination of Nepos but really to conquer the territory and add it to his own kingdom.

Already in the context of classical regicide enormous

divergences can be seen in the motives for killings too readily described by the blanket title 'assassination'. There is the sacrifice of the divine victim originating in the most primitive perceptions of kingship; there is the deliberate termination of power which has been misused to the point of insufferable tyranny; there is the murder of political rivals, and there is killing for factional interest or political expediency.

Kings and emperors may reign by hereditary succession; by the choice of the people; or by usurping the throne; but however they have acquired the crown or the imperial purple, they have in the past regarded themselves, and been so regarded by their subjects, as ruling by divine right. The murder of a king, therefore, has been an act of apparent self-exaltation on the part of common men, who have perceived a licence to carry out such an outrageous act only in the precedent of ritual killing, and in that narrow sense, *all* murders of kings can be seen as sacrificial acts.

The murder of Chosroes II, king of the Sassanid kingdom of Persia, by his son Siroes in AD 628, however, is interesting as a case of tyrannicide – the only form of assassination which has been regarded as justifiable in most serious thinking on the subject – and also of parricide, the form which has been most severely condemned throughout the ages.

Chosroes was indebted for his ascent to the Persian throne partly to Maurice, the Byzantine emperor who had been, by the standards of those times, a relatively wise ruler for twenty years. But in AD 602 Maurice was ousted by a military revolt led by a centurion, Phocas, who assumed the throne himself, supported by his troops. Maurice had promptly fled from Constantinople with his wife, their five sons and four daughters, to the port of Chalcedon, where he was captured. His five sons were killed one by one before his eyes, and then he himself was despatched. The heads of the six were struck off to be exhibited in Constantinople, and their trunks were thrown in the sea.

This atrocity provided Chosroes with an excuse for a crusade of vengeance. His Persian armies invaded Syria, Asia Minor and Egypt. He seized Jerusalem, Alexandria and the island of Rhodes, restoring to Persia the dimensions of its ancient empire and ruling it with despotic cruelty until the

Romans marched against him under Heraclius, and the hard-pressed Persians turned against Chosroes at last. His eldest son Siroes, learning that his father had appointed another son – his favourite – as his successor, overthrew Chosroes, massacred his other sons in his presence, and threw his father into a dungeon, where he died in a few days, possibly of starvation.

2

The Hollow Crown

Assassination (though not yet coined as a word) already had a venerable pedigree by the Middle Ages, but the killing of kings and emperors, which had been politically motivated in ancient Greece and Rome, took on decidedly religious undertones in the medieval period. One such was Wenceslaus, the 'good king' of Bohemia, who was murdered because of his Christianity. He was the elder of two sons of Uratislas, Duke of Bohemia, and his wife Drahomira. When his father died, his mother, who was a fanatical pagan, began a repression of Christians which stopped only when Wenceslaus, a man of intellect and Christian virtue, took charge of government himself as the next Duke of Bohemia. But his younger brother Boleslas was a pagan after his mother's own heart, and they formed a plot to rid the country of Wenceslaus and his religion, first murdering Ludmilla, the paternal grandmother of Wenceslaus who had brought him up as a Christian. Wenceslaus, meanwhile, was elevated to become King of Bohemia by Otto, the Holy Roman Emperor, and continued to defend the country's Christians against his mother's machinations. But he was too devout to be a strong ruler. One night whilst he was at prayer in his chapel, Boleslas came with six men and, creeping up on Wenceslaus as he knelt, one of them stabbed him in the back, the others then falling on him with their daggers. The killing was stupid and had the opposite effect to that intended. Otto marched into Bohemia with an army to avenge the death of the martyr-king and restored all Christian rights. Drahomira was executed and Boleslas, after being at first imprisoned, became a mere vassal ruler, subject to the Holy Roman Emperor and held in contempt by most of his people until his death.

Among the tribal assassinations of Anglo-Saxon England

were the murders of Aethelbald, King of Mercia, in 757; and Aethelred, King of Northumbria, in 796. Aethelbald, who had reigned in southern England for more than 40 years, seems to have been a tyrant who also fell foul of the Church because of his scandalous private life, and he was murdered by his own bodyguards near Tamworth. His death brought about civil war in Mercia, the outcome of which was Offa's ascendancy to the throne. Aethelred was King Offa's son-in-law, and his murder at the hands of his own courtiers brought an end to Mercian influence in Northumbria. Such treacherous violence was deeply shocking to the Anglo-Saxons, among whom loyalty to one's master was one of the cardinal principles of social order.

The crowns of pontiffs were no more secure than those of monarchs in those times. In 882 the elderly Pope John VIII, object of a conspiracy, was poisoned and then beaten to death by members of his entourage. Fifteen years later Pope Stephen VI was deposed, thrown into a prison, and later strangled by his enemies. Some say that Pope Benedict IV was assassinated by men hired by Berengar, the King of Italy, in 903, but there is no proof of that. Leo V, however, who succeeded him, was murdered in prison in 904 after a palace revolution led by one of his clergy, named Christopher, who proclaimed himself pope, but was soon overthrown and executed.

In 929 Pope John X died in mysterious circumstances, and was thought to have been murdered, probably by suffocation, in Castel Sant' Angelo, where he had been imprisoned after being deposed by a Roman woman called Marozia. (Some call her a Roman 'lady', but not I. Gibbon called her a prostitute!) She was a senatrix, head of the house of Theophylact, and virtually sole ruler of Rome. She had three noble or royal husbands, and was the mistress of Pope Sergius III. She appointed temporary popes to succeed John – Leo VI and Stephen VII – in order to place her bastard son by Sergius on the papal throne as John XI when he was old enough. The next pope was Leo VII, appointed by Alberic, Marozia's son and, according to some, also an offspring of Marozia. Later still the chair of St Peter was occupied by her grandson, Alberic's illegitimate son, the notorious John XII. Of him

Gibbon wrote that he 'lived in public adultery with the matrons of Rome; that the Lateral palace was turned into a school for prostitution; and that his rapes of virgins and widows had deterred the female pilgrims from visiting the tomb of St Peter, lest, in the devout act, they should be violated by his successor.'

The tenth century was a dangerous time to be supreme pontiff, but then the medieval popes were men ambitious for political and military power and Rome was torn by the rivalries of patrician families. John XIV was murdered in 984 at the instigation of the antipope Boniface VII, who had him poisoned, and who had also had another vicar of Christ, Benedict VI, strangled ten years earlier. Boniface may himself have been a victim of assassination in 985, in a palace coup. His corpse, at any rate, was exposed naked in the streets of Rome, where it was trampled and stabbed by the mob. Suspicion surrounds the death, also, of Pope Sergius IV in 1012. He seems to have disappeared from the Vatican during a fresh political upheaval in Rome, and Benedict VIII of the ruling family of Tusculum immediately took his place on the papal throne.

In 975 meanwhile, Edward, son of Edgar, had become king of the Anglo-Saxon kingdom of England. He was the son of Edgar's first wife, and was hardly more than twelve years old when he succeeded to the throne. He had an even younger half-brother, Aethelred, offspring of his father's second wife, Aelfthryth. Although the young king was popular, and relations between the three were ostensibly friendly, Edward's step-mother probably entertained the notion that her own son should be king. In 978 Edward paid a visit to his step-mother and his half-brother who were in residence at Corfe Castle. It seems that on his arrival at the gate, the king was greeted with due respect and ostentation by his brother's servants, but even before he had dismounted from his horse they suddenly seized him and stabbed him to death. One version of the story says that Edward tried to spur on his horse to make his escape, but, fainting in the saddle from his wounds, his horse dragged him along the ground as his foot became caught in the stirrup. The corpse was hidden in a well but, being found later, was buried at Wareham and thence taken to Shaftesbury Abbey, where – as with Wenceslaus's remains in Prague – miracles were ascribed to it, and the king came to be seen as a saint and has since been known as Edward the Martyr. Although it is generally believed that his murder was carried out at the instigation of his stepmother, there is no proof of this. At any rate, Aethelred succeeded his half-brother and has gone down in history as 'the Unready'.

Among the violent deaths of medieval kings that might be construed as assassinations are those of Duncan of Scotland in 1040 and William II of England in 1100. Shakespeare leaves schoolboys in no doubt that Duncan was treacherously murdered in his bed by Macbeth, urged on by his ambitious wife, and that Macbeth suffered from a guilty conscience afterwards, but in fact Macbeth, who had a legitimate claim to the Scottish throne, may have killed Duncan in battle. Duncan was regarded as a usurper by most of his subjects when he succeeded his maternal grandfather, Malcolm II, who was himself assassinated by his nobles in a conspiracy provoked by his high-handed actions. Malcolm had murdered the only other legitimate claimant, as he thought – the grandson of his predecessor Kenneth III. But the assassinated claimant had a daughter, Gruach, who became Macbeth's wife and gave him sufficient cause to challenge Duncan for the throne. Nevertheless, Shakespeare has apt messages for assassins, not only in Lady Macbeth's advice to her husband to 'look like the innocent flower, But be the serpent under't'; but also in warning of the inevitable state of mind after the deed is done, fearing discovery – 'if the assassination could trammel up the consequence . . .'

The death of William Rufus, usually regarded by historians as an accident, is open to more sinister interpretation. William succeeded to the throne of England in 1087 on the death of his father, William the Conqueror. He was a self-confessed adherent of the pagan religion, and was possibly homosexual. He came to the throne when he was about 30 and reigned for thirteen years. His oppression of the Church, and his quarrels with his elder brother Robert of Normandy, together with punishing taxation to pay for his wars and a series of poor harvests, not to mention his personal habits, combined to make him, as the *Anglo-Saxon Chronicle* put it, 'hated by almost all his people and abhorrent to God'.

On the afternoon of 2 August 1100, the king was hunting stags in the New Forest, possibly near Minstead (the exact site is uncertain), when he was killed instantly by an arrow shot by Sir Walter Tyrrell. The king's younger brother Henry was proclaimed king, forestalling the claim of Duke Robert. William's death was treated as an accident, and Tyrrell departed for Normandy without hindrance. But was it an accident? There are those who believe that William's death was a ritual sacrifice of a divine victim in the manner of the ancients, and that William was, as it were, an accessory to his own murder, accepting his fate philosophically in the tradition of the old religion and also accepting Tyrrell as his executioner. One account says that, when the arrow struck him, the king, without uttering a word, broke off the arrow's protruding shaft and then fell on his chest, hastening his death.

It seems more likely, perhaps, that he was a victim of political assassination. The future Henry I had entered into the quarrels of his two elder brothers, playing off one against the other, so that both of them distrusted him to such an extent that they entered into a treaty in order to disinherit him. If Robert should die childless, William would inherit all his lands in France. If William were to die childless, Robert would succeed him on the throne of England. Thus Robert had an interest in William's death. So had Henry. Robert was away on a crusade when the king was killed, and Henry was with the royal hunting party in the New Forest when it occurred. Tyrrell could have been an assassin hired by either of them, but more likely by Henry. The contemporary historian William of Malmesbury related that the king had had a dream the night before his death, in which he was being bled, and the blood spurted high into the heavens, blotting out the sky and turning day into night. There was also a story that a monk came to him on the morning of his death and told him that God intended his death in vengeance for his harsh dealings with the Church. The king is supposed to have laughed at this and said to Tyrrell, 'You do justice in this matter', to which Tyrrell replied, 'I will indeed, my lord.' William died on a Thursday and was buried in Winchester Cathedral next morning. Few mourned his passing. Henry was proclaimed king the same day.

If the ruthless Henry I suffered any attacks of conscience over this royal *coup d'état* we do not know of them, but Henry II's instigation of the murder of Thomas Becket was a different matter. Becket was the young king's friend. He had risen from obscurity to become Archdeacon of Canterbury, in which capacity he had been instrumental in securing Henry's succession to the throne on the death of Stephen. Within months of his coronation, Henry made Becket Chancellor of England. Becket's success went to his head, as frequently happens to those who rise to wealth and power from beginnings that fail to prepare them for it. The Chancellor outdid the king in worldliness and ostentation, but they remained close friends, hunting, drinking and playing chess together until Henry, for political reasons, proposed to make Becket his new Archbishop of Canterbury.

Suddenly Becket, who had hitherto managed the difficult trick of riding two mounts at once, astride the saddles of Church and State, made his choice and arguably backed the wrong horse. The man who as Chancellor had embraced the luxury of his exalted position with huge enthusiasm, and had been a ruthless warlord on the king's behalf in France, now as primate became an equally passionate ascetic, if that is not a contradiction in terms. He took to wearing a horsehair shirt, living on vegetables, and washing the feet of beggars in imitation of Christ. It was inevitable that the king's former friend should now become his opponent in the disputes between Church and State, chief of which concerned the extent of secular authority in administering justice. Becket defended the ecclesiastical courts against Henry's demands for paramountcy of the crown courts in enforcing the Common Law, and the archbishop became such a thorn in the king's side that he was eventually accused of treason and fled to the Continent, from where he excommunicated many powerful men close to the king. It remained expedient for the king to make his peace with his archbishop, however, and Becket returned to England, immediately excommunicating those who had officiated at the coronation of Henry's heir and namesake in Becket's absence. When the king was informed of this in

France, his temper exploded into the famous incitement, 'Will no one rid me of this turbulent priest?'

The hint was taken by four barons, who crossed the Channel and challenged Becket at Canterbury to restore order and save himself by lifting the excommunications and leaving England again. Becket refused, and, knowing that his time had come, behaved with bravery and dignity, going into his church and ordering the doors to be opened for his pursuers when they returned fully armed. The barons, FitzUrse, de Tracy, de Morville and le Brito, challenged Becket again at the altar of the Chapel of the Virgin Mary, and he again refused any concession or compromise, saying, 'In vain you menace me. If all the swords in England were brandishing over my head, your terrors would not move me.' They tried to drag him away, either because they intended at that point to arrest him or more probably because they feared to commit the sacrilege of killing him in the cathedral. But the archbishop resisted their attempts to remove him, and their heavy swords came down on his head and shoulders. It is believed that FitzUrse struck first, slicing off the top of Becket's head. The archbishop sank to the floor under the blows of the other knights, who struck him with swords and an axe, and then le Brito delivered the *coup de grâce*, bringing his heavy sword down with such force that it shattered Becket's skull and broke in two on the floor. Then a subdeacon, Hugh of Horsea, is said to have plunged a sword into the open skull and scattered Becket's brains and blood over the floor. This bloody execution, which took place on 29 December 1170, resulted in Becket's speedy if unworthy martydom. It was an example of what may be called expedient assassination.

The king, after acknowledging that his unguarded outburst had been the cause of the murder, and doing public penance by being scourged at the martyr's tomb, rode out the storm of protest throughout Christendom, but Becket's intransigence and his appalling murder together helped maintain the supremacy of Canon over Common Law in England for more than four centuries, until the Reformation. One of Pope Alexander III's conditions for Henry's absolution was a huge fine which would be used to finance a crusade to the Holy Land.

John of Salisbury, the scholar and cleric who was secretary to both Archbishop Becket and his predecessor Theobald, and who was wounded in the affray during Becket's murder, had written that the killing of a tyrant was in accordance with the will of God, and tyrannicide continued to dominate the philosophical justification of assassination. But whatever else Becket was, he was not a tyrant, and it was John of Salisbury who urged his canonisation on Rome.

The only true begetters of the name 'assassin', Hassan ibn-al-Sabbah's *hassasins*, were meanwhile carrying out their deadly operations in the Middle East, kings and princes of both Islam and Christendom being among their victims. The murder of the Wazir Nizam al Mulk at the instigation of the Sheik Hassan ibn-al-Sabbah in 1092 seems almost a prototype for the story of Henry II and Becket. The Wazir was a Seljuk statesman and leader of the orthodox Muslims whom the extremist Shi'ites opposed. He had been a boyhood friend of Hassan, but eventually political and religious differences led the Sheik to ask his devotees who would rid the state of the evil Nizam, and one of them stabbed the Wazir to death as he was being carried in a litter.

A hundred years later the Assassins, still highly active long after the death of the Old Man of the Mountain, murdered Conrad of Montserrat, crusader and king of the Latin kingdom of Jerusalem. They had disguised themselves as Christian monks and had passed as such for several months, ingratiating themselves with the crusaders until the opportunity to kill the king presented itself. They stabbed Conrad to death in church, in the town of Tyre, and tried to put responsibility for the murder on Richard I, saying they had been sent on their errand by the king of England. They were all executed.

Christian zealots, like Muslim ones, were as likely to be assassinated by the 'enemy within' as by the fanatics of an alien religion. In the thirteenth century Peter of Verona was murdered near Como. He was a Dominican who became a general inquisitor under Pope Gregory IX and was then made head of Innocent IV's newly established papal Inquisition, designed to exterminate remaining heretics of the Cathari or

Albigensian persuasion, whose opposition to Catholic doctrines had led to their suppression by one of the French de Montfort barons acting as the pope's general. But fierce opposition to the Inquisition had already led to the assassination in 1233 of Konrad of Marburg, who had tried to impose it on Germany, and in 1244 of the Toulouse inquisitor William Arnaud. In 1252 it was the turn of the papal inquisitor himself. Peter was returning to Milan from a preaching visit to Como when he was ambushed by Cathari supporters on the road, struck down with a blow from an axe, and then stabbed through the heart. He became known as Peter Martyr and as the patron saint of inquisitors, and in reaction to his murder Innocent issued a papal Bull which authorised the atrocities of torture and burning alive in the name of God.

Edward II was the next English king to fall victim to murder, in 1327. The homosexual king's twenty–year reign was a disaster for the country, and he was forced to abdicate at last by his queen Isabella, the 'she-wolf of France', and her lover, the Marcher lord Roger Mortimer. But lenient imprisonment of the deposed king at Kenilworth was not enough to satisfy the queen and Mortimer, who felt threatened by his very existence, and at length he was removed to Berkeley Castle, his head and beard being shaved so that he would not be recognised by anyone who saw him on the journey. His gaolers were apparently ordered to dispose of him without leaving a mark on his body. After attempting to starve him to death, but not having the patience to pursue this course, they murdered him by ramming a red-hot spit into his innards via his anus.

In 1389, Bartolomeo Prignano, Pope Urban VI, the probable instigator of several assassinations, was himself poisoned in Rome, having alienated everyone by his deplorable tenancy of the throne of St Peter, during which he was mentally unstable. He had occupied it for more than a decade and was 70 years old. His cruel tyranny and hypocrisy were infamous, and, as Gibbon wrote, he could 'walk in his garden and recite his breviary while he heard from an adjacent chamber six cardinals groaning on the rack'.

There is no proof that Richard II was murdered, as Shakespeare has it, although it does seem very likely. The continued

existence of a deposed monarch was always an embarrassment to his successor. Supporters of Richard whilst he was in
prison at Pontefract formed a conspiracy to kill the usurper,
Richard's cousin Henry Bolingbroke, as well as his four
sons. But the plot was discovered and the rebels rounded up
and executed. It seems virtually certain that Richard's fate
was thus sealed, and minutes of Henry IV's council accounts
lend force to the theory: 'To William Loveney, clerk of the
Great Wardrobe, sent to Pontefract Castle on secret business, by order of the king, 66s. 8d.' There is also strong
evidence that Henry suffered from a guilty conscience after
Richard's death. The probability is that Richard was starved
to death. Shakespeare's lament is apt enough:

> For God's sake, let us sit upon the ground,
> And tell sad stories of the death of kings:–
> How some have been depos'd; some slain in war;
> Some haunted by the ghosts they have depos'd;
> Some poison'd by their wives; some sleeping kill'd;
> All murder'd.

The theory of the divine right of kings – the 'Right Divine of
Kings to govern wrong', as Alexander Pope was to put it in
the *Dunciad* – was more or less abandoned as a formal notion
in England with the death of Richard II. But the principle was
long kept alive in France and other countries, and even in
Britain it survived in the collective unconscious, and in
certain conscious forms such as the royal touch for scrofula,
otherwise known as the 'king's evil'. The doctrine of divine
right was temporarily revived by the Stuart kings.

The preservation of the state was as much in the minds of
medieval kings as the outrage to their persons, however, and
Henry V's reaction to the plot against him uncovered on the
eve of his departure for France, in Shakespeare's version, was
the proper response to treason:

> You have conspired against our royal person,
> Join'd with an enemy proclaim'd, and from his coffers
> Receiv'd the golden earnest of our death;
> Wherein you would have sold your king to slaughter,
> His princes and his peers to servitude,

His subjects to oppression and contempt,
And his whole kingdom into desolation.
Touching our person, seek we no revenge;
But we our kingdom's safety must so tender,
Whose ruin you have sought, that to her laws
We do deliver you. Get you, therefore, hence,
Poor miserable wretches, to your death.

James I of Scotland knew how uneasy lies the head that wears a crown. He succeeded to the northern throne whilst in captivity in England, and was released on the promise of a huge ransom. James was reckoned to be one of the best-educated princes in Europe at the time, and as well as being a musician and a poet was also an athlete of note. But when he returned to Scotland as king, he resolved to give the war-torn country peace and strong government even if 'God gives me but a dog's life'. He brought with him as his bride Henry IV's niece Joan Beaufort, and part of his ransom was written off as her dowry. James swooped on the rapacious Scottish barons in his determination to bring law and order to the land and established constitutional monarchy in Scotland for the first time, but he made powerful enemies, and in 1436 a plot against him took shape among aggrieved barons and his own Stewart kinsmen.

At Christmas of that year, King James, 43 years old, went to stay with Dominican friars at Perth, and he was still there on 20 February when Sir Robert Stewart, the king's chamberlain, admitted Sir Robert Graham and eight other men into the convent. James was with his wife and her ladies-in-waiting when he heard them coming. In no doubt about what such a noise in a convent must imply, he quickly removed some floorboards and dropped into a space beneath, where he thought he could make his escape, but Graham and his men dragged the struggling king out and slaughtered him with their daggers, also wounding the queen as she tried to help her dying husband. The assassins were subjected to prolonged torture for their deed before they were finally beheaded. The intention of their sponsors to seize the crown was thwarted by the succession of James's six-year-old son to the throne.

Lesser mortals than kings disposed of in the meantime included in England – or at any rate in the English Channel – William de la Pole, the Duke of Suffolk. He had been largely responsible for organising the marriage of the feeble Henry VI and the redoubtable Margaret of Anjou, and he became the king's right-hand man, holding the fate of the country in his hands and feathering his nest at the nation's expense. It was rumoured that he had ordered the murder of Humphrey, Duke of Gloucester, the former protector, and he was held responsible for the loss of large parts of France which had been English possessions for three centuries. Impeached upon a multitude of charges including embezzlement, Suffolk was banished by the king, who thought thus to save the life of his favourite, but the ship carrying him to safety was intercepted and the duke thrown into a small boat where his head was unceremoniously hacked off with a rusty sword and chucked over the side.

The pattern of assassination was changing ominously from religiously inspired to politically motivated murder, replacing sacrifice for the sake of the people by sacrifice for the sake of a minority of the people, moved by personal greed, ambition and lust for power.

Italy, which had witnessed the murder of so many popes over the centuries, was also a major arena for assassination in the late fifteenth and early sixteenth centuries, but this time involving its more temporal princes. In 1476, at Christmas, Galeazzo Maria Sforza, Duke of Milan, was murdered, after ten years of cruel despotism, by Giralamo Olgiatti, who was executed believing he had won eternal fame by his deed. Two years later, in 1478, an illustrious member of the great Florentine Medici family fell victim to assassination. The rival Pazzi family, wealthy bankers of Florence, plotted to remove the brothers Lorenzo and Giuliano and themselves take over the government of the city. The proposed change of government had the wholehearted support of the pope, Sixtus IV, although he refused to condone the killing of the two Medici. But the Pazzi conspirators calculated that when the deed had been done, the pope would turn a blind eye. Lorenzo 'Il Magnifico', the grandson of Cosimo, founder of the family oligarchy, came very close to death when a clergyman member of the conspiracy put his left hand on Lorenzo's shoulder in the Duomo in Florence, to steady himself, whilst stabbing with his right hand. But Lorenzo's reaction to the touch was a lightning dodge which saved him as he defended himself from the blow with his arm. Lorenzo's brother Giuliano, however, was less fortunate. Four years younger than Lorenzo, he failed to escape the fate decided for him by the Pazzi and was brutally killed as his brother escaped. But the attempted coup failed. Medici supporters routed the conspirators, killing them all, and the members of the Pazzi family and other ringleaders were hanged and the Pazzi name disgraced.

Lorenzo's son and Giuliano's illegitimate son both became popes, as Leo X and Clement VII respectively, and it was the latter who commissioned Michelangelo's magnificent tombs of his father and uncle in Florence's church of San Lorenzo, and who refused to sanction the annulment of Henry VIII's marriage to Catherine of Aragon. But Leo X, Lorenzo's son, who had recently condemned Luther as a heretic, died suddenly in 1521 believing he had been poisoned. 'I have been murdered,' he said. 'No remedy can prevent my speedy death.' And none did.

A ruling family even more notorious than the Medicis for intrigue, murder and corruption was that of the Borgias. The already ageing Rodrigo succeeded Innocent VII as Pope Alexander VI in 1492, having bribed his way to the papal throne, and his sexual appetites and nepotism were such that, even in that permissive age, he brought disgrace on the Church, the prestige of the papacy scarcely ever sinking lower. He was himself implicated in several murders, including possibly – despite his exhibition of grief – that of Giovanni, Duke of Gandia, one of his own illegitimate sons, whom he may have wanted out of the way in order to favour another of his offspring, the notorious Cesare. The duke's corpse was discovered floating in the Tiber with several stab wounds.

Cesare Borgia's contemporary and champion, Machiavelli, was one of those who have argued in favour of the principle of assassination as a means to an end, and he wrote with approval of Cesare's own murderous acts of treachery, saying that 'cruelty is used well . . . when it is employed once for all, and one's safety depends on it, and then it is not persisted in but as far as possible turned to the good of one's subjects'. The sentiment was echoed by the Elizabethan poet Robert Greene:

> Why, Prince, it is no murder in a king,
> To end another's life to save his own:
> For you are not as common people be,
> Who die and perish with a few men's tears;
> But if you fail, the state doth whole default,
> The realm is rent in twain in such a loss.

In 1503, Pope Alexander sat down to dinner with his son Cesare and other cardinals at a banquet given by the Cardinal of Corneto. During the meal, he and Cesare were suddenly taken ill. Cesare, younger and with a stronger constitution, recovered, but the pope died, and although there is no proof it is believed by many that he was poisoned. Legend has it that a poisoned flagon of wine, intended for Cardinal Corneto himself, was switched and served to the Borgias instead.

An appalling example of treachery brought further mourning to the Medici family in 1537. Alessandro, Duke of Florence, was challenged by his kinsman, friend and drinking partner, the obscure Lorenzaccio de' Medici, to seduce a cousin of his, Caterina, a woman of known virtue, whom he offered to bring to his house one night and then leave them alone together. Alessandro readily entered into this arrangement. But what Lorenzaccio really had on his mind was tyrannicide. Many Florentines feared Alessandro's rule over their city, and Lorenzaccio saw himself as the delivering angel. 'Men do you harm,' Machiavelli had written a few years before, 'either because they fear you or because they hate you.' On the appointed night, Alessandro was waiting in bed for the arrival of Caterina when Lorenzaccio arrived, accompanied instead by a hired assassin named Scoroncolo. The two stabbed Alessandro in the throat and stomach and left him dying while they made their escape. Lorenzaccio was eventually stabbed to death in Venice.

Ten years later, Pier Luigi, son of another of the great

Italian family patriarchs, Alessandro Farnese, Pope Paul III, was assassinated. His father, the pope, had been educated at the court of Lorenzo de' Medici, and his aunt had been the mistress of Rodrigo Borgia, Pope Alexander VI. Alessandro Farnese had launched the Counter-Reformation, with the support of the Holy Roman Emperor, Charles V, but when he later distanced himself from Charles it was partly because the murder of his son at Piacenza seemed to be the result of a Habsburg conspiracy – after the killing Charles V had immediately taken possession of a duchy the pope had secured for Pier Luigi. The ensuing split between Alessandro and Charles was of some significance for the Catholic Church.

The heir to Edward IV was murdered in the Tower of London, along with his younger brother Richard, Duke of York. Oddly enough, the word assassination is rarely used in connection with the Princes in the Tower. But the murder in 1483 of the thirteen-year-old Edward V, by Richard III or his henchman Buckingham, was the last assassination – as opposed to execution – of an English monarch, and it is not without interest that an Italian visitor to Britain at the time, Mancini, wrote that the doctor from Strasbourg who attended the royal boy whilst he was in the Tower reported that 'the young king, like a victim prepared for sacrifice, sought remission of his sins by daily confession and penance, because he believed that death was facing him . . .'

The permanent removal of a young rival to the current top dog was not unique to Britain. In 1280 the child heir to the last Sung emperor of China had been murdered by the Mongols, and in 1591 the infant Dmitri, youngest son of Ivan the Terrible, died in mysterious circumstances, soon regarded as assassination at the hands of the boyar Protector Boris Godunov, who later came to the throne as Tsar of Muscovy.

3

So Excellent a King

In the sixteenth and seventeenth centuries, two murders of national leaders occurred which, if communications then had been as they are today, would have made instant headline news across the world. They were the assassinations of William of Nassau, Prince of Orange, and King Henri IV of France. All other assassinations of the period sink into relative insignificance beside these two, but let us look at some of them first.

In Turkey, the assassination of the presiding sultan's brother became almost a routine ritual like the ancient sacrifices of kings, but with political rather than religious motives. There was no established law of succession, so the elimination of potential usurpers was a device much resorted to by those who wanted to hold on to their power over the Ottoman Empire. Suleiman 'the Magnificent' had his eldest son Mustafa strangled in 1553, in order to make way for his offspring Selim by his favourite wife, the Russian slave Roxelana. It was scarcely a judicious choice – Selim was a debauched cardboard cut-out of a king, who left all decision-making to his ministers.

In Britain, meanwhile, the most notorious cases of the sixteenth century occurred in Scotland. In 1546 David Beaton, the Cardinal Archbishop of St Andrews and Chancellor to the young Mary Queen of Scots, was murdered in his chamber by a gang of Fifeshire lairds disguised as stonemasons. The archbishop cried out, 'I am a priest,' as they ran him through with their swords, then they mutilated his corpse and hung it naked from the castle's gatehouse. Beaton had ordered the execution, by burning at the stake, of George Wishart, the Protestant reformer, and the assassination was ostensibly in revenge for this. John Knox called this savage killing of Beaton a 'godly act'. But there was more to Beaton's death than just revenge. Beaton was the ecclesiastical leader of the opposition to Henry VIII's attempts to reform the Church in Scotland, and had opposed the king's plan to have Mary married to his son Edward. Beaton's assassins were supporters of the proposed marriage. They, of course, achieved nothing by his death.

The sordid intrigues surrounding Mary Queen of Scots are too well known to require detailed examination here. If David Rizzio, the queen's Italian musician and secretary, and possibly her lover, was brutally stabbed to death because of Darnley's jealousy, it was simple murder and has no place in this book. Only if Darnley had half-intended to kill her and the child in her womb, as Mary herself believed, and make himself King of Scotland, can the word assassination be used in this context, and it seems on the whole unlikely, even though the queen was actually threatened in the heat of the moment. Darnley himself was the victim of a conspiracy that misfired, or perhaps of more than one conspiracy. An attempt to blow him up in the house where he was staying in Edinburgh was found after the explosion to have failed, for Darnley's body was in the garden and he had been strangled. The motive and identity of Darnley's murderer are among the mysteries of British history, but Bothwell remains the chief suspect, despite his acquittal.

The enforced abdication of Mary led to the appointment of her half-brother James Stewart, Earl of Moray, as regent of Scotland, but he had been in office only six months when, riding through a street in Linlithgow, he was shot in the stomach with a musket from the upstairs window of a house belonging to John Hamilton, Archbishop of St Andrews. The regent managed to return to his lodgings, but died within a few hours. The assassin was a local laird, the archbishop's kinsman James Hamilton of Bothwellhaugh.

The murder of the Earl of Moray has an important significance in this history of assassination. It is the first I have so far discovered which was committed with the use of a firearm. The pistol, very soon, and then the revolver (not invented until the nineteenth century), were to become the favourite weapons of assassins through the centuries and worldwide.

Hitherto, the assassin had needed to be a braver man, willing to come into actual bodily contact with his victim in order to kill him (unless he resorted to the more sophisticated method of poison). As Machiavelli put it: '. . . princes cannot escape death if the attempt is made by a fanatic, because anyone who has no fear of death himself can succeed in inflicting it; on the other hand, there is less need for a prince to be afraid, since such assassinations are very rare'. The growing availability of convenient hand-guns undoubtedly increased the incidence of assassination. Firearms were compatible with the survival instinct of most assassins and multiplied the number of men who were willing to carry out killings of this kind, by allowing them to do the jobs at some distance, without blood physically reaching their hands and with less risk of being killed themselves in the process. The musket used to kill the regent of Scotland, and the pistol used in the first attempt on William the Silent in 1582, were the precursors of a new method of assassination that was to be challenged in effectiveness as a remote instrument of death only by the increasing use of terrorist bombs in the present century.

Although there were conspiracies to overthrow Mary Tudor, most notably the Wyatt rebellion of 1554, it does not seem that the queen's assassination was ever envisaged. When one man, William Thomas, *did* suggest that the queen should be 'slain as she did walk', the idea was turned down by his fellow-plotters, and after the capture and imprisonment of the traitors Thomas tried unsuccessfully to commit suicide by 'thrusting himself under the paps with a knife'.

In 1570 came the first of many plots against Elizabeth I, all of which, though their primary object was to depose the Protestant queen and replace her with a Catholic monarch, would inevitably have involved her assassination or execution. If any of them had succeeded, of course, the event would have resounded throughout the world as the murders of William the Silent and Henri IV were to do. This first conspiracy against the English queen was engineered by a Florentine businessman, Roberto Ridolfi, who was in league with the Spaniards and intended to put Mary Queen of Scots on the English throne. But Elizabeth, in common with all the

Tudors, had an efficient intelligence network, and the plot was discovered and dealt with before it really got off the ground. The fourth Duke of Norfolk was among the conspirators and was duly executed.

Pope Pius V had declared Elizabeth a heretic, and his successor, Gregory XIII, gave his and the Catholic Church's blessing to anyone who would assassinate her. But some of the candidates for the honour were simpletons or madmen, like John Somerville, a Warwickshire gent who set off for London with the intention of killing her, because she was a 'serpent and viper' and he wanted to see her head on a pole. But he foolishly boasted of his intention to some people he met on the road, and was soon incarcerated in the Tower where he committed suicide after his trial for high treason.

Francis Throckmorton was the next and more serious messenger of death to the queen. Sir Francis Walsingham, Elizabeth's Secretary of State, who ran her 'certain curiosities and secret ways of intelligence', uncovered a conspiracy which Throckmorton was helping to organise at home and abroad. Walsingham's men followed him for six months and then pounced, throwing him into the Tower where he was tortured on the rack until he confessed to the large-scale plot for a Catholic army to march on London, and named those involved, including Mary Queen of Scots, the Earl of Northumberland and the Duke of Guise in France, who was enlisting the help of Spain. The treason was efficiently crushed.

Suspicion and distrust were the orders of the day in Tudor government. 'Whoso taketh in hand to frame any state or government ought to presuppose that all men are evil. . .' Sir Walter Raleigh wrote, and government spies were everywhere, listening to whispered plots. When Polonius advises Laertes in *Hamlet* to 'Give every man thine ear, but few thy voice', he was speaking only what every politically conscious person knew perfectly well. Erasmus had said that 'bad monarchs should perhaps be suffered now and then. The remedy should not be tried,' and he warned that '. . . kings have many ears and many eyes. . .' It was advice that both Catholic and Protestant conspirators in the Tudor age should have learned from the Bible: 'Curse not the king, no, not in thy thought; and curse not the rich in thy bedchamber; for a bird of the air shall carry the voice, and that which hath wings shall tell the matter.' (Ecclesiastes 10:20).

Soon it was discovered that Dr William Parry, a Member of Parliament, was planning to kill the queen. A Catholic who wavered in his loyalties, Parry had apparently become convinced that it was honourable to kill a monarch who had been excommunicated, and he intended to shoot her in the head with a pistol when she was riding in her coach. The Tudors made political capital out of this plot, as of others. There are grounds for suspecting that much of the supposed swell of treason during the Tudor period was well-organised propaganda designed to bring the reigning monarch the public's sympathy and support – a device that was to be used by Hitler's Nazis, among others. Richard Walpole wrote in 1599 that the world was growing 'over well acquainted with these tales of Queen-killing'.

In the case of Parry, the government characterised him as a man of base parentage, who led a wasteful and dissolute life, who had deflowered his step-daughter and attempted to murder a creditor, and who had only been saved from the death penalty for that offence by the queen's personal clemency. He was really a Catholic gentleman and a lawyer, but the propaganda brought strong justification and public support for the sentence passed on him, which was that he be 'hanged and let down alive, and thy privy parts cut off, and thy entrails taken out and burnt in thy sight, then thy head be cut off, and thy body divided in four parts. . .'

Anthony Babington was the chief participant in the next conspiracy. He wrote indiscreetly to the imprisoned Mary Queen of Scots at Chartley Castle, in Staffordshire, asking her to say whether he and his supporters should free her before murdering Elizabeth, but Mary replied that it would be preferable for Elizabeth to be killed first, and by thus committing her thoughts to paper Mary signed her own death warrant, for the correspondence was intercepted by Walsingham. Babington and several other ringleaders were convicted of treason and executed, being partly hanged, cut down whilst still alive, then castrated, disembowelled and quartered.

Elizabeth had not merely approved of such savage treatment but had virtually recommended it. She had no qualms of conscience about this punishment of disloyal subjects, but she shared with them moral uncertainties about the killing of a sovereign which derived from the ancient reverence and superstition about the divinity of monarchs that we have observed. There was much soul-searching among some of Elizabeth's potential assassins about the deed they were contemplating, and Elizabeth was so reluctant to be seen authorising the execution of the Queen of Scots that she suggested to Sir Amyas Paulet, who had Mary Stuart in his custody, that he might do away with her in secret. When he refused, saying 'God forbid that I should make so foul a shipwreck of my conscience. . .', the queen threw scorn on his 'daintiness'.

Ludicrous plots were still being hatched, with Philip of Spain's encouragement, to assassinate Elizabeth in her old age. In 1594 Dr Lopez, a Portuguese physician, was executed for allegedly forming a conspiracy to poison her, and three years later, Edward Squier, a seaman, was captured by the Spaniards and persuaded by the Inquisition to kill her. He attempted to do so by spreading poison on the pommel of her saddle, but it failed to work, no doubt because the queen did not lick her fingers.

During all this intrigue in the court of Elizabeth of England, Philip II of Spain had been widely suspected of the assassination of his son and heir, Don Carlos, whose mother had died a few days after giving birth to him. The young widowed Mary Queen of Scots had had designs on Carlos as a prospective husband, for the sake of the Spanish throne rather than for any longing for the prince himself, for Don Carlos was deformed, lewd, sadistic and possibly insane, and an embarrassment to Spain and its image abroad, especially after Philip had married Elizabeth of Valois, the daughter of Henri II of France, to whom Carlos himself had been betrothed. But the story seized upon by Schiller, Verdi and others that the prince had a passion for his step-mother has little foundation in fact, as Carlos was only a boy when the marriage contract was made and then broken. Nevertheless, it is true that the Infante hated his father, was in league with

Spain's Protestant enemies in the Netherlands, and was alleged by Philip to have plotted against his life.

In January 1568 the king and some officers arrested Carlos in his bedroom in the Alcazar in Madrid and imprisoned him. The prince seems to have been convinced that they had come to kill *him*. He had regularly slept with swords and pistols close at hand, but the king advanced this fact as evidence that his son intended parricide. At any rate, some months afterwards Don Carlos was dead, and the date and manner of his end are still shrouded in mystery. One account says that he was fed with poisoned broth and that his death was kept secret for several months. Another says that four slaves killed him, three of them gripping him by his arms and feet while the other strangled him. The official version, naturally, was that he had died of an illness. But there seems little doubt that Philip had him murdered, with the tacit approval of the Inquisition.

That Philip was well able to contemplate such an act is shown by the fate in 1570 of Florence de Montmorency, Baron of Montigny. He was a Netherlands envoy to the Spanish king. On his last visit he was prevented for months by Philip from returning home to the Netherlands, and was at last imprisoned in Segovia and put on trial for his life, though on what charges no one could discover. He was at first sentenced to be executed by beheading, as the Count of Egmont and Montigny's brother Hoorn had been not long before, but there was some fear that the execution of another distinguished nobleman of the Netherlands might have adverse effects on Spain. Instead, Montigny was removed to a fortress at Simancas, and there a treacherous doctor was very publicly brought to attend him, telling the curious that Montigny had a fatal illness. Then, a few days later, in the middle of the night, Montigny was garotted, and it was put out that he had died a natural death as a result of his disease. Philip of Spain had planned the murder meticulously to avoid any suspicion of foul play, and the truth was only confirmed long afterwards with the examination of Philip's correspondence.

Charles IX of France is also believed by many to have been assassinated during this period. The third son of Henri II and Catherine de' Medici, he was a useless monarch who died

39

young in 1574, two years after the St Bartholomew's Day massacre to which he had given his assent under pressure from his mother. It is believed that poison was spread on the pages of a book he was reading, and that he, unlike Elizabeth I, ingested it by his well-observed habit of licking his fingers to turn over the pages.

The murder of William the Silent, if it did not change the course of world history, certainly had major implications for Europe in the sixteenth and seventeenth centuries, and some of its effects are still with us. William, Count of Nassau and Prince of Orange, was the hero of the Netherlands' fight for freedom from Spanish domination and the architect of the Dutch republic. Brought up as a Catholic but later embracing Protestantism, he led the revolt of the Dutch people against Philip of Spain's persecution, particularly after the Spanish Inquisition declared the entire population of the Netherlands to be heretical and showed it was prepared to deal with it accordingly, hanging all those who showed any inclination whatever towards the new religion. William was a nobleman of rare qualities; not only a military commander of genius and a statesman of rare wisdom and tolerance, but a man of great moral courage and intellectual gifts from whose lips, it was said, no arrogant or indiscreet word ever fell. But he was a rebel leader, the enemy of the Catholic King of Spain, and consequently of the Church of Rome, and there was a price of 25,000 écus on his head. Five attempts on his life were made on behalf of the Spanish tyrant before the one which succeeded in 1584.

In March 1582, one Juan Jaureguy, a Catholic youth, discharged a pistol at the prince at such close range that, passing through his neck from under the right ear and coming out under the left jawbone, the shot set William's hair and beard alight. Momentarily blinded and stunned, but still on his feet, the prince's first words when he recovered his senses were 'Do not kill him', but it was too late. The culprit had immediately been run through by the swords of the prince's attendants. When they emptied the dead man's pockets, there were two dried toads and pieces of hare skin as well as a crucifix and other items. William believed his end had come, but devoted care by his physicians and attendants secured his recovery, the latter keeping the wound closed by continuous pressure of their fingers, in relays, night and day, for seventeen days.

Later in the same year, one Basa, an Italian, and Salseda, a Spaniard, were arrested on suspicion of planning to poison the prince, and confessed that they had been hired to do so by the Duke of Parma, commander of the Spanish forces in the Netherlands. Basa committed suicide in prison, but Salseda was taken to Paris and tried. Being found guilty, he was torn to pieces by four horses tied to his limbs.

In March 1583 one Pietro Dordogno attempted to kill the prince, and confessed before his execution that he had travelled specially from Spain with that end in mind. A year later a Dutch merchant named Hanzoon was executed for making two attempts to blow up William, in the prince's house at Flushing, and in church. He confessed that he had been encouraged to carry out the deed by the Spanish ambassador in Paris. Then a Frenchman named Le Goth obtained his release from prison by promising his Spanish captors that he would kill the prince by poisoning his food, but he then went to William and told him the story.

During the whole period of these various attempts on the life of William the Silent, one man had been trying to create the opportunity for his own ambition. Balthazar Gérard was a young French Catholic fanatic, a cabinet-maker's apprentice. With the blessing of the Duke of Parma, he inveigled himself into the Prince of Orange's service by pretending to be one Francis Guyon, a Calvinist, whose father, he said, had been martyred in the Protestant cause. William gave him twelve crowns to buy himself shoes and clothing, but instead he bought two pistols from one of the prince's own guards.

On 10 July 1584, William was at Delft where he enjoyed a private dinner at the Prinsenhof with his family and one guest, the Burgomaster of Leeuwarden. As they left the table, William paused outside the doorway of the dining room to speak to an officer, and at that moment Gérard stepped forward and shot him, the balls passing through William's lungs and stomach. '*Mon Dieu*,' he gasped as he sank into the arms of an officer, 'have mercy on my soul. My God, have mercy on the poor people.' He was dead within minutes, and had no time to think or say anything about his murderer. Captured as he tried to escape through the garden, the assassin was executed in public four days later, his right hand being first burnt off with a red-hot iron, then flesh being torn from his body with pincers, and finally, his body being quartered and disembowelled and his heart flung in his face before he was beheaded. William the Silent would never have countenanced such barbarism, but he was so beloved of his people that nothing that could be done to Gérard was nearly enough punishment for the man who had robbed them of their national leader. 'As long as he lived,' J. L. Motley summed it up, 'he was the guiding star of a whole brave nation, and when he died the little children cried in the streets.'

Philip of Spain rewarded Gérard's parents for their son's deed. The soldier who had sold Gérard the pistols in good faith committed suicide when he learned how they had been used. Elizabeth I of England, who had been giving under-cover support to the Protestant rebels for some time, while maintaining a pretence of neutrality, now came out into the open and stepped up English aid, throwing down the gauntlet to Spain. The defeat of the Spanish armada four years after William's death was of immense help to the Dutch struggle.

William of Orange's aim had been to unite the whole of the Spanish Netherlands into one independent nation. If he had lived he might have achieved it, but without him there was no chance, and the northern Protestant territories, the United Provinces, were split off from the southern Catholic region we now know as Belgium. The assassination of William the Silent did thus influence the course of European history, but at the same time, Maurice of Nassau, William's son and successor, made the Dutch army into one of the finest in Europe and drove the Spanish out, establishing the independence of the United Provinces. One might suppose, then, that William's death would at least have established for potential assassins of all time the First Law of Assassination: the treacherous killing of one who is revered by most of the people will always have the opposite effect to that intended, by strengthening the resolve of the majority to achieve his purposes and resist violent change.

Philip II had had the support of the Catholic King of France, Henri III, against the revolt of the Netherlands, but religious turmoil in France was giving that country its own problems in the meantime, and among others three members of the powerful house of Guise were murdered between 1563 and 1588. The Guise family were powerful feudal lords, and Catholics of an opposing faction to the king, who was weak and ineffective, a 'painted, wincing sodomite' who, as Duke of Anjou, had been seriously considered as a potential husband by Elizabeth I, notwithstanding his violent anti-Protestantism and the fact that she was nearly twenty years his senior. The Guises were largely responsible for the Huguenot persecution during the wars of religion in France, and François of Lorraine, second Duke of Guise, was shot in the back by a Huguenot named Poltrot in 1563, during the siege of Orleans.

In 1588, the third duke, Henri, was murdered at Blois by order of the king, and his death was followed next day by that of his brother, Cardinal of Lorraine and Archbishop of Rheims. The duke had headed the Catholic League which had conducted a reign of terror against the Protestants of France, and he had become so powerful and ambitious that he threatened to displace the king himself, especially when events rendered a Protestant, Henri of Navarre, the king's heir. When the king decided to rid himself of these two troublesome noblemen, rumours of a plot actually reached the duke but he ignored them. Two days before Christmas, Henri III issued ten of his bodyguards, the so-called *Quarante-Cinq*, with daggers, and ordered mass to be said for their success. The duke was summoned to the king's bedchamber in the castle, where he was stabbed repeatedly by the conspirators. He staggered across the room to the foot of the king's bed, streaming blood across the floor, and there fell dead. Next day the archbishop was similarly disposed of in an attic.

The assassinations served no useful purpose and did Henri no good whatever. He was excommunicated for murdering a cardinal and was denounced from Catholic pulpits as an assassin, a heretic and an infidel. A few months later he was murdered by a Catholic fanatic, a Dominican friar named Jacques Clément, who stabbed the king in the abdomen and was immediately killed himself, after being asked rhetorically, 'Dare you look an angry king in the face?' and answering, 'Yes, yes, yes! And kill him, too!'

Henri III was the last of the Valois kings of France, and was succeeded by his brother-in-law Henri of Navarre, the first of the Bourbon dynasty, who became Henri IV. He was a Huguenot but on his accession embraced Catholicism, as the majority religion of his country, in his attempt to restore to the crown its former dignity and authority. With the Edict of Nantes he secured a degree of religious tolerance and he brought peace and prosperity to France at last under his absolute but benevolent rule. Henri IV was much loved by his people. So when he, too, was murdered, in 1610, France made of the murderer, François Ravaillac, an 'example of terror' that would, it thought, 'convert all bloody-minded traitors from the like enterprise'. They called it the *amende honorable*.

Ravaillac, another fanatical Catholic, who had evidently believed that the king was about to make war against the pope, was a schoolmaster and part-time secretary who was subject to 'visions'. He was first bound supine on the scaffold and the hand which had held the murderous knife was burnt off with flaming brimstone. Then the executioners used red-hot pincers to sear his nipples and tear out pieces of flesh from his thighs, arms and other fleshy parts of his body, and poured scalding oil, pitch and brimstone into the wounds, then molten lead into his navel, all the while exhorting the wretched, shrieking Ravaillac to reveal the names of his accomplices. The executioners finally tied his limbs to four horses, and drove them away so that they should dismember him, but had to sever the sinews with a knife before the horses were able to tear the arms and legs from the trunk, whereupon the frenzied mob fell upon the bloody carcass and continued to beat it and cut it up until there was scarcely anything left of Ravaillac but bones.

The French public, stunned by the death of their 'good

father', refused to believe that the murder was the act of a fanatical individual. It must have been a conspiracy – by the Jesuits; the Catholic League; the Spaniards; or someone else. If it was, it never came to light. But there had been nine other attempts on the life of Henri before this one, and it is as well to bear in mind that kings are potential sacrificial targets from the moment of their accession, because of what they *are*. It is much the same for republican heads of state, as royal surrogates, whereas mere politicians become targets only because of what they *do*.

John Knox was far from being the only cleric to try to justify assassination in the sixteenth century. It was a much-debated question then. Those who strove to vindicate assassins were mostly Catholics who argued that it was a holy deed to rid the people of an heretical ruler. One such was the Jesuit Juan de Mariana, who wrote a treatise in Catholic Spain asserting that it was justifiable for any man to kill a ruler who was a tyrant, or otherwise evil, in accordance with the wishes of the people. But his views outraged countries with less religious and political stability than Spain had at the time, for de Mariana's words were seen as an incitement to any discontented citizen to take the law into his own hands. Indeed, he had approved of the assassination of Henri III of France. After the murder of Henri IV, de Mariana's book was publicly burnt in Paris by the common executioner.

Across the world, in a China that was untroubled by the moral fastidiousness of European Catholic and Protestant thinkers, T'ai-Ch'ang, emperor of the decaying Ming dynasty, is believed to have been poisoned as a result of a court plot against him in 1620.

In France, another notable victim soon followed the king to the grave, notwithstanding all precautions and deterrents. Concino Concini, a Florentine friend and attendant of Henri IV's widow Marie de' Medici, now regent and pro-Spanish, was entrusted with power by the queen mother and, as Marquis d'Ancre, appointed Marshal of France. His wife was one of Marie's maids, Leonora Saligai. It was Concini who first brought Richelieu into the French government. But the unstable condition of the country and Marie de' Medici's divisive policies led to fierce opposition and widespread hatred, and Concini and his wife, the deformed maid, soon became notorious for their grasping corruption and prodigality. On 24 April 1617, Concini was murdered – shot outside the Louvre by conspirators who had been organised by the timid young king, Louis XIII, urged into action by his favourite, the Duc de Luynes. Hardly had Concini been buried than the Paris mob dug up his corpse and hung it up by its heels from a gibbet on the Pont Neuf, after gutting it and cutting off the testicles, and danced around it as if possessed by devils.

The death of George Villiers, Duke of Buckingham, is frequently referred to as assassination, although it was clearly murder, even if half the nation would willingly have participated in it. Villiers was a handsome young man with whom King James I fell in love at first sight and raised from menial servant to a dukedom within seven years. He became one of the richest and most powerful men in the kingdom and won the confidence of the young Prince Charles as well. It was Villiers who organised the fateful marriage of Charles to Henrietta Maria, and when he led the nation into pointless wars with France and Spain there was a threat that he would be brought to trial for treason. He was a divisive influence between king and parliament and was thus partly responsible for the Civil War.

As Buckingham left the breakfast table at his house in Portsmouth, on 23 August 1628, a Suffolk man, John Felton, drew a long knife and thrust it 'with great strength and violence, into his breast and under his left pap, cutting the diaphragma and lungs, and piercing the verie heart itself. The duke, having received the stroke, instantlie clapping his right hand on his sworde hilt, cried out, "God's wounds, the villaine has killed me!"' Felton, who was mentally unbalanced, steadfastly maintained that he had committed the act for the public good, and the killing did save other lives, for Buckingham had been about to resume a military campaign in France, having already lost half his men on the previous expedition. But the king was appalled by the public rejoicing at the duke's death, and Felton was hanged at Tyburn. Even Buckingham's coffin had to be protected from the cheering crowds at his funeral.

During the Thirty Years War in Europe, Count Albrecht von Wallenstein, an able mercenary soldier and the richest nobleman of Bohemia, raised a private army to fight for the Habsburg emperor Ferdinand II, who made Wallenstein a prince of the Holy Roman Empire and rewarded his victories with the duchies of Friedland and Mecklenburg. But Wallenstein's very success was his undoing. He became too rich and powerful for the comfort of the emperor, who suspected Wallenstein of planning to take the crown of Bohemia for himself and so arranged to have him removed in 1634. At first the conspirators plotted only to take the general prisoner, but this plan was soon changed when it became apparent that a sudden revolution might ensure Wallenstein's liberty. Wallenstein's chief assassin was an Irish officer of his own army, named Deveroux, who burst into the general's bedroom with his henchmen and challenged Wallenstein as a traitor before he and the others ran him through with their halberds.

In Britain, meanwhile, the failure to assassinate any monarch after the young Edward V had not been for want of trying. The various abortive plots against Elizabeth I were followed by the Gunpowder Plot against James I and the equally well known Rye House Plot against Charles II.

Cromwell, who was offered and refused the crown, was also the target of several assassination plots, most notably the conspiracy of Colonel John Gerard, who was executed on Tower Hill for his attempt in 1654. Royalist plots to overthrow Cromwell were wisely tempered by uncertainty as to the public reaction – a caution which a great many of history's conspirators would have been well advised to emulate. Gerard, however, sought to overthrow the government by chopping off its head, as it were. He intended to seize Cromwell, with the aid of thirty men, as the Protector travelled from Whitehall to Hampton Court by road, but as efficient spies and conscience-stricken informers have protected English monarchs from assassination, so they preserved the Lord Protector. (One plot was abandoned because the getaway horse caught cold!) 'Walls have ears' was a proverb which apparently originated in the seventeenth century. Cromwell travelled by river instead, and the conspirators were not arrested until the following day, as if Cromwell intended to turn the plot into propaganda by gaining sympathy when it was realised how close he had apparently been to death by treachery. Two of the conspirators were executed and three transported.

The period was still seeing much agonised moral debate about the justice of killing tyrants and despots. John Milton's *The Tenure of Kings and Magistrates* of 1649 had asserted that 'it is lawful to call to account a tyrant or wicked King and after due conviction to depose and put him to death. . .' This tract was written, of course, to justify the execution of Charles I, but in 1657 a pamphlet entitled *Killing No Murder* came into the country from Holland and recommended the assassination of Cromwell. It was written by a Royalist convert, Colonel Edward Sexby, who himself failed in an attempt to kill Cromwell in the year of the pamphlet's appearance.

The public at large would have been as shocked by Cromwell's murder as by the king's execution, for as Macaulay wrote, the English 'regard assassination, and have during some ages regarded it, with a loathing peculiar to themselves'.

The Scots, however, were not so scrupulous, and in 1696 an elaborate Jacobite plot to assassinate William III was formed with the tacit approval, if not indeed the express direction, of James II, to be backed up by a new Jacobite rising to take over the country once it had been accomplished. The assassination plot's chief engineer was Sir George Barclay, a Scottish Catholic who recruited a miscellaneous gang of forty, the plan being to ambush the king after his regular Saturday hunting in Richmond Park. The king always crossed the Thames at the same spot and returned via Turnham Green, and there the conspirators planned to await him, some of them appointed to deal with guards and outriders whilst Barclay and eight companions were to stop the coach and kill the king. But when the appointed day came, Saturday, 15 February, William decided not to go hunting, because the weather was unsuitable. The conspirators waited for the following Saturday. But in the meantime, the tension proved too much for some of the less resolute assassins, and the plot was betrayed. The king cancelled his hunting plans on the next weekend also, and the few assassins who had not hastily deserted on learning that the word was out, thought of murdering the king at Hyde Park Corner when he was on his way to chapel on the Sunday. But this all came to nothing, some of the conspirators having already been arrested and the others making themselves scarce. Most of them were eventually caught and executed at Tyburn, and the Jacobite Plot, long in gestation, was stillborn.

4

Revolution and Revenge

In 1712 Jonathan Swift was in the company of Robert Harley, first Earl of Oxford, when the Lord Treasurer received a parcel in the post that both men thought suspicious. Swift opened it, with extreme caution, to find two pistols inside that were arranged to go off when the recipient took off the lid of the box quickly. It was the second attempt to assassinate Lord Oxford. A few years earlier a French emigré named Guiscard had tried to stab him with a penknife.

These experiences of his friend did not prevent Swift from satirising the paranoid tendency of governments to suspect treason and employ spies to seek it out in every dark corner. When the hero of *Gulliver's Travels* visits Balnibarbi, a professor at the academy there shows him 'a large paper of instructions for discovering plots and conspiracies against the Government. He advised great statesmen to examine into the diet of all suspected persons; their times of eating; upon which side they lay in bed; with which hand they wiped their posteriors; to take a strict view of their excrements, and from the colour, the odour, the taste, the consistence, the crudeness, or maturity of digestion, form a judgment of their thoughts and designs: because, men are never so serious, thoughtful, and intent, as when they are at stool: which he found by frequent experiment: for in such conjectures, when he used merely as a trial to consider which was the best way of murdering the king, his ordure would have a tincture of green; but quite different when the thought only of raising an insurrection, or burning the metropolis.'

One of the first kings of the eighteenth century to die by treachery was Nadir the Conqueror, Shah of Persia, the 'King of Kings' whose tyranny was avenged in 1747 by an assassin whom the Shah called 'You dog!' as he died. Ruling Persia was to be a dangerous occupation in modern times, as monarchic absolute rule survived there when it was gradually becoming a thing of the past in many other parts of the world. Similarly, the removal of Prince Dimitri in Russia set the stage for the constitutional policy of that country, as described by a German diplomat – 'absolutism tempered by assassination'. Sir Francis Bacon had long before observed that suspicion disposed kings to tyranny. And as tyranny also disposed men to conspiracy, tyranny and assassination lived in a self-perpetuating partnership.

In France, meanwhile, the exemplar of terror provided to the nation by the execution of Ravaillac proved to be no ultimate deterrent. In 1757 Robert François Damiens pushed past two guards and tried to stab Louis XV as the king was stepping into his carriage at Trianon, but succeeded only in wounding him under the fifth rib. The king thought at first that someone had punched him, but then felt the blood, and when he had been taken indoors he felt faint and thought he was dying. The queen and their daughters fainted on entering his room and seeing him covered in blood. But examination showed that the wound was not deep and the only fear was that the assailant's knife might have been dipped in poison, which proved not to be the case. The king duly recovered.

Nevertheless, Damiens was condemned to make the *amende honorable* in the Place de Grève in Paris, and suffered almost identical torments to those of Ravaillac, at the hands of the public executioner Sanson. 'My God,' Damiens kept repeating, between his shrieks and groans, 'have pity on me! Jesus, help me!' In France they still upheld the doctrine of the divine right of kings long after it had been abandoned as a formal concept in England, and saw Damiens' attempt on the king's life as the only crime more heinous than regicide – parricide. Damiens was a 42-year-old former footman, who had been employed in the homes of Parlement officials and had often heard the king being denounced by his masters. As Voltaire put it: 'The monster is a dog who has heard a few dogs of the Enquêtes barking and has caught rabies from them.' But few believed that Damiens had acted alone. Some thought he was the agent of the Jesuits, others that his instigators were the Jansenists. Damiens admitted nothing, even under the most horrific cruelties. He insisted that he was moved to act as he did by the king's conduct towards the French parliament, which was, in truth, deplorable. The clerk of the court, Monsieur le Breton, kept going up to the wretched victim after each new torment and asking him if he had anything to say. Damiens said each time, as long as he was conscious, that he had not. He was finally torn apart by horses, as Ravaillac had been, after Sanson had cut through his thighs with a knife.

Five years later, Peter III, Tsar of All the Russias, was strangled to death at Ropsha four days after being forced to abdicate in favour of his wife, Catherine. 'Not enough,' he said, 'to prevent me reigning over Sweden and tear the crown of Russia from my head. They must have my life as well.' The killing was carried out, probably at Catherine's bidding, by one of her lovers, Count Orloff, and other officers, who claimed to have been drunk at the time and afterwards told the Tsarina that they could not remember what they had done. She, meanwhile, ascended the throne as Catherine II, sometimes called 'the Great'. Soon afterwards, in 1764, Ivan VI, son of Ivan V's daughter Anna, was murdered after spending most of his life in solitary confinement from the time when Peter the Great's daughter Elizabeth had become Tsarina in 1741.

Catherine the Great attempted to by-pass her son Paul, whom she hated with some justice, by naming her grandson Alexander as her successor. But Paul had her will destroyed and took the crown himself. One of his first acts was to bring his father's remains to St Petersburg to be buried with due ceremony, and he forced Peter's assassins, Count Orloff, Prince Potemkin and the Princess Caterina Dashkova, who had played a leading role in the plot, to walk in the snow behind the funeral procession. Paul was epileptic, tyrannical, and arguably insane, and after a few disastrous years of his rule a small group of men headed by Count Pahlen made up a deputation to ask him to abdicate for the sake of the country. He was about to declare war on Britain in collaboration with Napoleon, though Russia was near bankruptcy. The conspirators brought a document effecting the abdication to Paul in his bedroom at the Mikhailovsky Palace at St Petersburg.

When he refused to sign it, he was strangled there and then. Napoleon tried to blame the death of his ally on the British. The official version was that he had died of apoplexy. His son and successor, Alexander, had some knowledge of the plot to depose his father, though just how much is not clear. He was shocked but took no steps to punish his father's murderers. The death of Paul I, at any rate, was a ritual sacrifice in the classic mould.

Meanwhile, in 1791, Potemkin had died, possibly also by assassination. Grigori Alexandrovich Potemkin had been a rival of Count Orloff in the affections of Catherine (one of the 'many called' and 'many chosen', as Pushkin described her procession of lovers). He had risen to a powerful position in the Russian court, but his ambition led him into overreaching himself, and his death at 51 was reputed to be as a result of poisoning.

Alexander's policies were responsible for the assassination of August von Kotzebue at Mannheim in 1819. Kotzebue was a prolific German dramatist and author, and a friend of Beethoven – Beethoven had composed the incidental music for Kotzebue's plays *King Stephen* and *The Ruins of Athens*. Kotzebue held various posts in the Russian service and suffered from divided loyalties. He had been exiled from the Weimar Republic when he was twenty, and from Russia to Siberia under Paul I. His opposition to the liberal tendencies of the German government became well known through his publication of an anti-democratic weekly journal, and he was identified as being an agent of the Tsar. During a period of student unrest in the universities, when they were being branded as hotbeds of revolution, Kotzebue became a target for the students' venom. In March 1819, he was stabbed to death by Karl Ludwig Sand, a member of a radical student organisation from Jena. Sand had been involved in a public burning of Kotzebue's books and had planned for six months to kill him. As soon as he had done so, he rushed out into the street and twice wounded himself with a dagger in attempts to commit suicide, whilst shouting patriotic slogans. He was imprisoned for more than a year, then executed by decapitation, and the only outcome was much stricter control of political activity in German universities.

In the following year in France, the Duc de Berri, Charles

Ferdinand, was shot by a man named Louvel as he left the Paris Opéra one night with his pregnant wife Caroline, daughter of Francis I of Naples. 'Blessed Virgin, have mercy,' the dying Catholic duke said. He had long had designs on the French crown (and so had the duchess, for that matter), but French hatred of the aristocracy soon put paid to his chances, if they ever existed.

In Abyssinia, King Joas was assassinated at the instigation of the King of Tigré, Michel Sohul, who took control of the country himself, but was soon overthrown.

King Gustavus III of Sweden had been murdered in March 1792 by a Captain Jacob Anckarström, who shot him during a midnight masquerade at Stockholm's opera house. The king died a few days later. The rule of this monarch, who was intellectual and highly-strung and had a preference for the young pages in his court rather than the ladies, had become despotic, though the king introduced religious liberty, freedom of the press and other liberal reforms. He was described as a 'strange mixture of . . . cold-blooded intriguer, high principled hero, and unworldly aesthete'. There had been a mounting aristocratic conspiracy against this generally enlightened monarch who had jeopardised his country's finances by declaring war on Russia.

Events further west were to dominate the world stage for the last years of the eighteenth and the first decades of the nineteenth century. In 1793 occurred a killing which most would put down as one of history's half dozen most famous assassinations, but which I maintain was murder, though it was unquestionably a symbolic sacrifice. Jean Paul Marat, one of the leaders of the French Revolution, hero of the people and champion of universal suffrage, had contracted a hideous and painful putrefying skin disease known as prurigo whilst hiding in Paris cellars and sewers during the turmoil leading up to the declaration of the republic. His body was covered in running sores and he gave off a repellant stench of decay. He could obtain relief only by sitting in a warm bath, wrapped up in towels, and he was doing so when Charlotte Corday was admitted to his residence at 44, Rue de l'École de Médecine in Paris on 13 July 1793.

The 25-year-old beauty who had travelled to Paris from Normandy to see him was really a woman of noble birth, Marie Anne Charlotte Corday d'Armans, and a Girondist. The Girondists were the political opponents of Marat's radical Jacobins, but Corday told Marat that she had come as a spy to give him information on the Girondists' treasonable activities at Caen. Citizen Marat began to make notes as she spoke, and as he did so she drew a knife she had bought earlier that day and plunged it into his breast, piercing a lung and severing the aorta. '*A moi, chère amie,*' cried the dying Marat, and Corday was quickly overpowered by those who rushed in to Marat's aid, too late. Not that Charlotte Corday resisted arrest. She proclaimed her guilt at once. The 'angel of the assassination' was executed on the guillotine four days later in the Place de la Revolution. A Paris doctor named Sue wrote afterwards that 'one of the executioners held up her head by her beautiful hair and slapped the face in front of the crowd. The face, which was pale, had no sooner received the slap than both cheeks visibly reddened, and her countenance expressed the most unequivocal marks of indignation.'

'I killed one man,' she had said, 'to save a hundred thousand; a villain to save innocents; a savage wild beast to give repose to my country.' But she was deluded in this belief. She had evidently acted entirely alone; she was no part of any plot or conspiracy to kill Marat, and I do not see that this personal act should be dignified by the title of assassination. Any individual who plans the death of another, whether king or commoner, and carries it out alone, turns himself or herself into judge, jury and executioner, and lacks the justification of shared convictions, whatever may be said in support after the event. In fact, far from bringing repose to France and saving innocent lives, Corday's murder of Marat contributed to the unleashing of the Terror, which resulted in the deaths of about 17,000 victims. It was an example of what might be called symbolic assassination. It achieved no good, and probably did a great deal more harm than if Marat had been left alone. As it was, he became the revered martyr of the revolution – this former doctor who had once said: 'In order to ensure public tranquillity, two hundred thousand heads must be cut off.'

The killing of the Shah of Persia in 1797 was an entirely different matter. Agha Mohammed Khan had seized the throne by force and subjected the city of Kerman to an appalling massacre, demanding seventy thousand pairs of eyes to be brought to him to satisfy a blood-lust which even the Roman emperors might have balked at. The eyes were delivered to him on dishes. He was murdered by his own attendants, and not a minute too soon.

A plan in October 1800 to assassinate Napoleon, by stabbing him in his box at the Paris Opéra – a plot which the French thought had been engineered by the British – might have served a useful purpose if it had succeeded, but the Bonapartes, as it turned out, seemed immune to assassination. Napoleon I survived several attempts on his life. When Saint-Rejeant, Carbon and de Limoelan tried to blow Napoleon up with an infernal machine in the Rue Saint-Nicaise, on his way to the Opéra on Christmas Eve of the same year, his life was saved by his drunken coachman, who set off down the road at a gallop. A plot in 1804 against Napoleon's life *was* backed by the British. The plan was uncovered by French police, who believed the Duc d'Enghien to be the leader of the conspiracy, and he was convicted and shot.

Suspicions that Napoleon *was* assassinated, when he died on St Helena at the age of 51, derive partly from the will he dictated there just before his death, in which he took a last swipe at the old enemy by saying, 'I die before my time, killed by the English oligarchy and its hired assassins.' There is often an element of religiously inspired fantasy in the suspicions of murder which have followed the deaths of greatly revered men who die young or against expectation, as happened with Alexander the Great. But there is no mystery at all about the death of Napoleon. A post mortem was carried out, in accordance with his own wishes, and he was shown to have died of stomach cancer.

Aspiring British assassins could not dispose of their own leaders, let alone anyone else's. There were several attempts on the life of the fairly inoffensive George III by isolated madmen seeking some private gratification. The king assumed on each occasion that his assailant was out of his or her mind. Whether this was due to a conviction that only a madman would attempt to kill a reigning monarch, or to a rare insight resulting from his own fragile state of mind, is open to question. In 1786 a woman named Margaret Nicholson attempted to stab the king as he alighted from a carriage. She was seized immediately and the king, unharmed, said, 'Do not hurt her, for she is mad.' This was, in fact, true, and she was committed to the Bethlem Hospital for life.

The most famous attempt on George III's life occurred at the Theatre Royal, Drury Lane, in May 1800. His Majesty had just arrived in the royal box for a performance when an ex-soldier, James Hadfield, fired twice at him with a pistol. Both shots narrowly missed their target, but, the man having been arrested and no one hurt, the king asked for the performance to go on as if nothing had happened, and was apparently so little agitated by the incident that he fell asleep during the interval. Hadfield, it turned out, had received permanent brain damage from a sword penetrating his skull when he was serving in Flanders. He believed he was called upon by the Almighty to sacrifice himself for the sake of the world, but not by suicide, so a curious logic had persuaded him to do so by killing the king.

'An attack upon the king,' said the Lord Chancellor at Hadfield's trial, 'is considered to be parricide against the state, and the jury and the witnesses, and even the judges, are the children. It is fit, on that account, that there should be a solemn pause before we rush to judgement.' It was sound advice, not always heeded since. Hadfield followed Margaret Nicholson to Bethlem, and the case led to changes in the law which provided for the more enlightened treatment of criminal lunatics.

John Bellingham, who harboured a grievance against the government, had been hanged when he succeeded in killing the Prime Minister, Spencer Perceval, in 1812. He went to the House of Commons and shot the Prime Minister at point-blank range as Perceval was walking through the lobby.

'Murder!' the Prime Minister cried as he fell. It was his last word, and it was an accurate one. Of course there were immediate suspicions of conspiracy and insurrection, but this was not assassination. Nevertheless, the case has some significance as it raised important legal questions of criminal responsibility, which were only answered about 30 years later when Daniel MacNaghten, a Glasgow man, shot Edward Drummond, the Prime Minister's secretary, in mistake for the premier himself, Sir Robert Peel. MacNaghten was acquitted of murder on the grounds of partial insanity proposed by his defence counsel, and after the trial a lengthy debate in the House of Lords brought into being the so-called MacNaghten Rules. These laid down that to establish a defence on grounds of insanity it must be proved that, at the time of the act, the accused did not know the nature and quality of the act he was committing; or, if he did know it, he did not know that what he was doing was wrong. It was a very imperfect formula, but it served the law in Britain and other countries for more than a century.

Five years after the death of Spencer Perceval, in January 1817, the much-despised regent, the Prince of Wales, was attacked as he was riding along the Mall to Carlton House after opening a new session of parliament. Stones were thrown, and a hole was found afterwards in the window of the coach. It was assumed to have been made by a shot from an air-gun, and the prince himself certainly thought an attempt had been made to assassinate him.

In 1820, the Cato Street Conspiracy was uncovered, which had plotted to overthrow the government by assassinating the entire Cabinet. Its leader was Arthur Thistlewood, a ne'er-do-well who proposed to establish himself as president of the new republic which he imagined would be welcomed with open arms by the public after the success of his armed insurrection. The heads of Lord Castlereagh and Lord Sidmouth were to be cut off and paraded through the streets in triumph. But it was Thistlewood and his partners in crime who lost their heads, in more ways than one. The plot was betrayed, the conspirators arrested, and the five ringleaders were hanged and then decapitated.

William IV was enjoying the racing at Ascot in 1832 when a

former sailor with a wooden leg threw a well-aimed stone at him, hitting him on the forehead but causing no serious injury. That any attempt to injure a monarch was still regarded in Britain as such an unbelievably heinous atrocity that it could only be perpetrated by a madman is evidenced by the committal of this offender, John Collins, to a lunatic asylum. He had stated in court that he did it because he had lost his leg in action, had been refused a pension, and was starving to death.

In 1847 the first of the numerous attempts to kill Isabella II of Spain occurred. Court intrigues were the hallmark of her reign, which began when she was three, but no one succeeded in removing her until she abdicated in favour of her son, Alfonso.

The Habsburg Emperor Franz Josef of Austria-Hungary also escaped an attempt to kill him in Vienna in February, 1853, five years after he had come to the imperial throne aged eighteen. He was unpopular with most of his people, and a Hungarian named Janos Libényi succeeded in wounding him with a knife, but the emperor survived until he was 86, becoming one of the longest-serving rulers of modern times, in spite of several other plots against him.

In January 1858, an attempt was made on the lives of the Emperor Napoleon III – Bonaparte's nephew – and the Empress Eugenie, as they were just arriving at the Paris Opéra. It was not the first attempt to kill the French emperor. More than one plot against his life had been foiled before, and in 1856 three Italians, named Tibaldi, Grilli and Bartoletti, had been arrested in Paris for an attack on him whilst he was visiting his mistress, the young Countess Virginia di Castiglione. The emperor's coachman managed to beat off the attackers and drive off to safety, and at their trial the three men, along with other conspirators, charged with attempted parricide, implicated the Italian republican Mazzini in the conspiracy.

The author of the 1858 plot was Count Felice Orsini, an Italian patriot who had been one of Mazzini's lieutenants and believed that Louis Napoleon had betrayed Italy after the destruction of the Roman Republic. He and his accomplices carried out a bomb attack which succeeded in inflicting only the most trivial injuries on the emperor and empress, but killed eight other people and a few horses and wounded more than 150 people, blinding some. The emperor and empress both showed great courage in ensuring that attention was given to the wounded before they departed, Eugenie dismissing concern for her safety, saying, 'It is our business to be shot at.'

Orsini and three other Italian revolutionaries, named Pieri, Gomez and Rudio, were arrested for the crime. Orsini had used bombs manufactured in Birmingham, and travelled to France on a British passport in the name of Thomas Allsop. Britain was criticised by the French for sheltering foreign refugees and failing to prevent such conspiracies. The incident led to Palmerston's resignation as Prime Minister when, trying to amend the law to meet this criticism from across the Channel, he was defeated on the grounds of preserving English liberty. Orsini and Pieri were guillotined; Gomez and Rudio sentenced to life imprisonment.

Danilo II, Prince of Montenegro, was murdered two years later, and I use the word 'murdered' advisedly. Danilo Petrovic Njegos became ruler of his small country (now part of Yugoslavia) at the age of 25, and, though autocratic, he achieved some useful reforms, as well as defeating Turkish invaders, and he made Montenegro into a hereditary principality, establishing secular rule instead of the religious supremacy in government which had been in force since the sixteenth century. But after only nine years Danilo was shot, at Persano in August 1860, by a man whom he had exiled, after a revolt against him by warlike tribesmen who were dissatisfied by his generally pacific foreign policy. He died two days later and was succeeded by his nephew, Nicholas.

Some years earlier in Italy, a Vatican minister, Count Rossi, had been stabbed in the neck by a sculptor, Sante Constantini. He died instantly. It was six years before a tribunal brought those responsible to justice. The leader of the conspiracy, which supported demands for more liberal government in Rome, was Colonel Grandoni of the National Guard, and he and Constantini were sentenced to be executed, but the colonel hanged himself in prison. Several other conspirators were sent to the galleys.

The taste for killing kings or other heads of state, meanwhile, had crossed the Atlantic. In January 1835 a lunatic named Richard Lawrence tried to kill President Andrew Jackson, but twice failed to discharge his pistols, apparently due to dampness. Lawrence was an English decorator in Washington who suffered from delusions of grandeur, believing that he was Richard III, with estates in Europe and large financial claims on the United States government which the President, in concert with certain steamship companies, was preventing him from laying his hands on. After the failure of his pistols, the second of which he fired at point-blank range, the President set about Lawrence with his walking stick and knocked him unconscious. Lawrence spent the rest of his life in mental hospitals. This was an instance of what might be called paranoid assassination.

A much more interesting matter, for most people, is the mental state of John Wilkes Booth. Abraham Lincoln was the sixteenth President of the United States, and was 56 years old when he went with his wife and their two guests to Ford's Theatre in Washington, on 14 April 1865, to see a performance of *Our American Cousin* by Tom Taylor. It was Good Friday. The President had begun his second term of office six weeks earlier, and only a week before the Civil War had ended with the surrender of the Confederate forces under General Robert E. Lee. The theatre visit was in the nature of a celebration.

The guests Mr and Mrs Lincoln took with them were Major Henry Rathbone and his fiancée Clara Harris, and they sat at the front of what in Britain would be called the 'royal box', with the President and his wife behind them. During the third act of the comedy, Booth opened the door of the box, stepped inside, and shot the President in the head at point-blank range with a Derringer pistol. The ball penetrated Lincoln's brain and lodged behind his right eye. The play stopped immediately and there was great commotion in the theatre. Major Rathbone tried to overpower Booth, but was seriously wounded in the arm by a slash from Booth's knife, and the assassin, crying 'Sic Semper Tyrranis' (Thus die all tyrants) – a sentiment that would have seemed absurd to anyone who understood it – then leapt from the box on to the stage, but caught a spur in the curtain as he jumped and crashed to the boards, fracturing an ankle. Nevertheless, he managed to get away and make his escape on a waiting horse.

People in the theatre were screaming. The President, unconscious but still alive, was carried to a tailor's house across the road and laid on a bed to await the arrival of doctors, who could do little to help him. Abraham Lincoln fought to survive for some hours, but died just after seven the next morning.

Booth had escaped with a companion, David Herold, trying to elude pursuing Union soldiers by heading south into Maryland, then crossing the Potomac into Virginia and finally hiding in a barn, where they were cornered by troops twelve days after the murder. Herold surrendered but Booth refused, and the soldiers set fire to the barn. One shot was fired, and Booth died from a bullet in the head. It is not known for certain whether he committed suicide or was shot by a soldier. A Union sergeant claimed to have killed him.

There had been more than 80 threatening letters treated as assassination plots against President Lincoln, and he had had a recurring dream about being assassinated, in which he saw a corpse lying in state in the White House and, on enquiring who was dead, was told by a soldier, 'The President. He was killed by an assassin.' Nevertheless, like Caesar, Lincoln tended to dismiss warnings and elaborate precautions to protect him, saying, 'If it is God's will that I must die at the hands of an assassin, I must be resigned so to die.' On another occasion, Lincoln said: 'If they kill me, the next man will be just as bad for them; and in a country like this, where our habits are simple, and must be, assassination is always possible, and will come if they are determined upon it.' Two years before his death, a hundred-thousand-dollar reward was offered by a group of Lincoln's Southern opponents to anyone who would kill him.

The question is, who were 'they' on the night of Lincoln's shooting? John Wilkes Booth was an actor, the son of Junius Brutus Booth, who had played the classics at Covent Garden and Drury Lane and rivalled Kean himself before emigrating to America. John's older brother was Edwin Booth, the first American actor to gain an international reputation as a tragedian. John was in many ways an attractive personality, but undisciplined, and some saw his most outrageous performance as an act inspired by jealousy of his more famous brother, whom he thus upstaged for all time. It is conceivable that this element was present in the depths of Booth's mind, and his choice of the theatre as the scene of his performance lends weight to this idea. More to the point, though, are the facts, first that there was a history of mental illness in his family, and secondly that Booth himself claimed he was avenging the Confederacy, believing that Lincoln had rigged the voting to get himself elected and intended to proclaim himself king.

Booth did not act alone, but the conspiracy was his own conception and his associates were a motley crew. One was Lewis Paine, a former Confederate soldier and subsequently a vagrant with several aliases. Another was the said David Herold, unemployed and mentally deficient. They met in the boarding-house of Mrs Mary Surratt, whose son John was involved, and where a German ferry-boat operator named Atzerodt lodged. They were sometimes joined by two of Booth's old school friends, named Arnold and O'Loughlin. Booth originally planned, before the end of the Civil War, to kidnap Lincoln and hold him to ransom for the release of Confederate prisoners, and two attempts to do so were frustrated by last-minute changes in the President's movements. When the war ended, Booth plotted instead to kill Lincoln as well as Vice-President Andrew Johnson and Secretary of State William Seward. Booth would deal with the President at Ford's Theatre, while Paine shot Seward and Atzerodt shot Johnson at their respective homes.

In the event Atzerodt lost his nerve on the appointed day and did nothing. Paine gained admittance to Seward's house and went berserk with a knife, wounding the Secretary of State, his two sons, a male nurse and an attendant, some of them seriously. But only Abraham Lincoln died, and Andrew Johnson became President in his place. Paine, Herold, Atzerodt and Mrs Surratt were hanged. O'Loughlin and Arnold were sentenced to hard labour for life, along with Dr Samuel Mudd, who had treated Booth's injured leg during his bid for freedom. Edward Spangler, a stage-hand at the theatre who was alleged to have assisted Booth's escape, was given six years. John Surratt escaped abroad. It seems almost certain that Mrs Surratt, at least, was entirely innocent of any involvement in the crime, and there was a good deal of disquiet about her execution.

The assassination threw Americans into a frenzy of doubt and enquiry which has never subsided completely. Appalled by the death of their father-figure, like the Dutch in 1584 and the French in 1610, they overreacted, not only in dispensing 'justice' but also in seeking further scapegoats. There were (and remain) suspicions about the part Edwin Stanton, Lincoln's Secretary for War, played in the affair, and some have regarded him as the real author of the plot, while others have tried to implicate General Ulysses S. Grant, who was invited to accompany the Lincolns to the theatre, but backed out, and among others suspected have been Andrew Johnson, the secret service, and the Jesuits. The man who arguably *should* have been hanged, however, was John F. Parker, a police constable on the White House staff who was detailed to be Lincoln's bodyguard for the evening of the theatre visit. He was supposed to sit in the foyer outside the door of the President's box, but when Booth came to carry out the murder, Parker had deserted his post and gone to the bar for a drink.

Lincoln's assassins never deluded themselves that they were sacrificing one man for the sake of all the people. They were, as with the murderers of Julius Caesar, acting, so they thought, on behalf of one political party, in this case the southern states. But this was a delusion, too. The death of Abraham Lincoln was a tragedy for the whole of the United States. The first Republican President's policies died with him.

5

Presidents and Potentates

The second half of the nineteenth century was a dangerous time for national leaders of all kinds and in all parts of the world, but especially in Europe, where the period saw the rise of an epidemic of anarchism which threatened all authority. Kaiser Wilhelm I, Bismarck and King Alfonso XI of Spain joined Franz Josef and others in surviving assassination attempts. Bismarck was attacked by one Kulmann in July 1874. The Kaiser, who had been the target of Oscar Becker in 1861, was shot at twice within a fortnight in 1878. After the second of these occasions he claimed that the man responsible, an anarchist called Nobiling, who seriously wounded him, was in fact the 'best physician I ever had', for the incident seemed to stimulate the Kaiser, who was in his eighties and frail. He lived on for another ten years.

Queen Victoria was like a cat with nine lives, as far as would-be assassins were concerned. Over a period of forty years she survived a surprising number of efforts to end her life. In June 1840, during one of her many pregnancies, she and Prince Albert were riding in an open carriage in London when a youth named Edward Oxford fired twice at her with pistols. Both shots missed. People in the crowd shouted 'Kill him!' Oxford was at first committed to Newgate pending a charge of high treason, amid speculation about a Chartist conspiracy or an Orange uprising, but he was later confined to Bethlem and Broadmoor, spending 27 years in care before he was released.

Two years later, an unemployed carpenter named John Francis apparently tried to shoot the queen as she was again riding in a carriage. This time police and the queen's escort were prepared, since both the prince consort and another person in the crowd had observed, the day before, a man holding a pistol. The queen deliberately went out again to lure him into the open. Francis was condemned to death for high treason, but was reprieved and transported instead, when it was accepted that the pistol was not loaded! Prince Albert took the view that if Edward Oxford had been flogged on the previous occasion, this later assault would not have happened. The crime was undoubtedly imitative of Oxford's, but no plea of insanity was made on Francis's behalf. The queen's own attitude was rather less merciful than that of George III, her grandfather. She recoiled emotionally from the idea of the death penalty, but considered it a necessary evil. If it had been carried out, Francis would have been first hanged, then decapitated and quartered.

Various other incidents which are often counted as assassination attempts were not really so, being merely assaults with no murderous intent. But a serious attempt to kill the queen was made in 1882 when she was at Windsor railway station. A young man fired at her with a revolver, narrowly missing his target, and he was about to fire again when two Eton College boys set about him with their umbrellas, and he was quickly arrested. The man was Roderick Maclean, and he was charged with high treason, but was soon shown to be mentally defective, and was sent to Broadmoor. The then Prime Minister, Gladstone, remarked to Her Majesty, as if it were a comforting thought, that whereas assassins in other countries had political motives, in England they were always madmen. In fact, though, Gladstone's history was shaky and his logic wrong – mad men or women now posed a much greater threat to kings because the spread of democracy was reducing the risk of murder of constitutional monarchs from political motives.

There were still a few absolute rulers and despots to be removed by those who believed in violent methods, however, Political murder in the volatile Balkan states included that of Michael of Serbia in 1868. Mihailo Obrenovic was the most enlightened of modern Serbia's rulers, and had freed the country from the grip of the Ottoman empire, but his murder at the age of 44 was provoked by his despotism in the internal government of the country.

In the next decade the sultan of Turkey, Abdul Aziz, who

had been deposed and sent into exile after a *coup d'état*, was found lying dead in a pool of blood, in June 1876. Knowledge of his murder could have brought further violence and possibly civil war to Turkey, so the government put it about that he had committed suicide, and imported a host of foreign doctors to back up this story.

Aziz was succeeded by Murad V, but only a few days after the death of his predecessor, the new sultan's ministers were also victims of a bloody massacre, when an army officer named Hassan shot his way into a Cabinet meeting. He shot and wounded the War Minister, Hussein Avni Pasha, before another minister, Ahmed Kaisserli, grappled with him, but was wounded with a knife. All the other Cabinet ministers had meanwhile made themselves scarce except one Raschid Pasha, who remained terrified in his chair. Hassan next attacked the wounded war minister again, this time with his knife, and killed him. Then he shot Raschid. Two more officials and a police officer were also killed before Hassan was overpowered. The Turks suspected that the massacre was a prelude to a Russian-inspired coup, and Hassan was brutally tortured, but the official story put out was that he had gone mad. That did not stop them from executing him, of course – the McNaghten Rules had not reached as far as Turkey.

Spain had its troubles in this period, and in 1869 the cathedral of Burgos was the scene of a shocking assassination that seemed like Becket's in reverse – instead of a spiritual authority being murdered by temporal assassins, a temporal figure was murdered by priests. The northern city of Burgos, where the Spanish national hero El Cid was buried, boasted the finest Gothic cathedral in the country. Señor de Castro, the city governor, was opposed to interference by the Church in state affairs. In January, 1869, he went to mass in the cathedral, and several priests drew knives from their cassocks and stabbed him to death whilst he was kneeling in prayer. They were all brought to justice.

The liberal Prime Minister of Spain, Marshal Juan Prim, was the victim of a murderous attack by right-wing extremists in the following year. He had placed on the Spanish throne Amadeus, Duke D'Aosta, the King of Italy's son, who was highly offensive to Spain's Catholics, having put an end to the temporal powers of the Vatican. Shot as he was riding in a carriage, Marshal Prim was only wounded, but a finger had to be amputated and it became seriously infected, resulting in his death. King Amadeus soon beat a retreat back to Italy, but so far from changing the history of Spain, the episode was merely one among many incidents in the country's crisis of monarchy.

Five years later, the President of Ecuador, Gabriel Moreno, was murdered by three members of a secret society opposed to the president's corruption and tyranny. The President was both stabbed and shot in a corridor of the palace at Quito. One of the three responsible, named Rayo, was killed by guards immediately, but the others escaped. The assassination failed to achieve the desired results.

As for the killing of the Viceroy of India, Lord Mayo, in 1872, that in no way qualifies as assassination at all, though it is often described as such. The earl was simply murdered by Shere Ali, an inmate of a convict settlement in the Andaman Islands, following an official inspection. The convict regarded Lord Mayo as the representative of an unjust system by which he was imprisoned. He had originally been sentenced to death for killing a relative in an hereditary blood feud, but the sentence had been commuted to life imprisonment. Ali, however, regarded a family feud as being outside British jurisdiction. Neither the killer nor his fellow-convicts can have imagined that the murder would achieve any beneficial change in their condition. He had done it by the order of God, Ali said, as he went back to the death cell.

The year 1881, on the other hand, brought two public killings which were altogether more sensational in countries far apart and not yet aspiring to world power – America and Russia. In the spring of that year, the Tsar of All the Russias, Alexander II, was killed by a bomb, and in the summer the United States President, James Garfield, was shot dead.

The principal issue at stake during Alexander II's reign was the ending of serfdom, and the Tsar brought this about with the Emancipating Act of 1861. Yet he was murdered by agents of the left in Russia. The reason was that he was liberal not by nature but by necessity. Rumblings of revolt would have grown into the full thunder of revolution much earlier than they actually did if Russia had not cast off the feudal structure of its society at that time. But Alexander remained absolute monarch of a state which his government could not change fast enough nor rule efficiently for the benefit of the people. The lot of the peasants was not much improved by their 'freedom'. The growth of revolutionary groups, some non-violent and others advocating terrorism to achieve sweeping reforms, resulted in several attempts on the Tsar's life, beginning with that of the communist student Dimitri Karakosov, who tried to shoot him in 1866. In the following year a Pole named Beregowski fired a shot at him in Paris as he was riding in an open carriage near the Bois de Boulogne with the Emperor Napoleon III. The bullet missed both emperors, hitting a horse and wounding a woman spectator. Beregowski was sentenced to life imprisonment. In 1873 a terrorist named Alexander Solovyev also tried to shoot the Tsar but failed.

These would-be assassins were all apparently acting alone, and Karakasov and Solovyev were executed, but their failed attempts gave impetus to the desire of militants to get rid of the Tsar as the symbol of all that was wrong with Russia. Over the next few years, revolutionary groups tried to blow up the Tsar in his train, in the streets, and in the Winter Palace at St Petersburg, but all attempts failed for one reason or another, and it was left to a nihilist group, led by Andrei Zheliabov, to do the job that many now saw as a necessity.

Zheliabov formed a terrorist committee called the People's Will, and on 13 March 1881, three of its members carried out the next attack on the Tsar. Alexander was riding home in an open carriage with an escort of Cossacks. Ironically enough, he had just signed a document heralding some minor consti-tutional changes. Sophia Perovskaia, one of the leaders of the People's Will movement, signalled with her handkerchief to two of her comrades as the Tsar's carriage approached. One of them, Rysakov, threw a bomb. It missed the carriage but wounded several Cossacks. Alexander got out of the carriage, and the other terrorist, Grimievetsy, then threw a bomb at the Tsar's feet. The explosion tore Alexander apart, but he lived for over an hour.

What the People's Will group thought was a case of sacrificing one man for the sake of the people turned out to be nothing of the sort. Like the murderers of Caesar, they mistook the man for the movement. The result of the killing was severe reaction and repression by the new Tsar, Alexander III. Tolstoy wrote to him pleading for clemency for the three assassins and three other leaders of the terrorists who had been condemned to death. Admitting that the terrorists, because of the 'imaginary good they seek, must wish to kill you too', and understanding the Tsar's desire to avenge his father's murder, Tolstoy nevertheless argued that if Alexander were to pardon the killers 'the hearts of thousands, of millions, will throb for joy and tenderness at this example of goodness shown from the throne at a moment so terrible for the son of a murdered father'. Alexander, however, was unmoved. He could pardon an attempt on his own life, he replied, but he did not have the right to pardon the murderers of his father. All six were hanged, and many other terrorist leaders were rounded up and either executed, sent to Siberia, or incarcerated in the Schlüsselburg Fortress. The mass of the people stood by and looked on while the new Tsar (who survived two assassination attempts a few years later) established his own autocratic rule.

We have noticed enough examples of this type of error of judgement, often by well-meaning rebels, to formulate what we might call the Second Law of Assassination: any killing that is inspired by hatred of the victim, if he is in a position of unassailable power, is liable to be a political error, since he will be replaced by someone else who pursues precisely the same policies and may be even more zealous than his predecessor. Better the devil you know than the devil you don't know.

Alexander II had ruled Russia for 25 years when he died. James Garfield survived for only six months as President of the United States, and if the Tsar's death was in any sense a tragedy the murder of the President was in some ways a comedy. Charles J. Guiteau shot Garfield in the back in the waiting room of a railroad station where the President was due to catch a train for his summer vacation. The President died eleven weeks later. Although Guiteau claimed he wanted to restore the right wing of the Republican Party to power after Garfield had followed the liberal faction, there is no doubt that the man acted alone and was out of his mind, and this killing should not therefore be called assassination but murder. Guiteau claimed that the killing was an act of God, and it turned out that he had written a speech for the Republican candidate which, though it was not used, he felt had been instrumental in Garfield's election. Entitled to some reward for his part in the President's success, therefore, he asked for the job of United States ambassador to Austria, then for a consulship in Paris. He had told his father at one stage that he was 'in the employ of Jesus Christ & Co., the very ablest and strongest firm in the universe'. Several members of his family were of doubtful mental stability. An uncle died insane and two cousins had been committed to asylums. Guiteau's sister claimed that, although her brother had wounded the President, the shot that killed him had been fired by someone else, hidden in a dark doorway. Guiteau revelled in the limelight during his trial, and although he pleaded insanity and was backed up by expert witnesses, he was declared guilty and sane by the jury, and hanged, shouting out on the scaffold, 'Glory hallelujah! I'm going to the Lordy!'

The year following the Russian and American murders was the one in which the Phoenix Park murders were committed in Ireland, when Lord Frederick Cavendish, Secretary of State for Ireland, and T. H. Burke, Permanent Under-Secretary, were ambushed by Irish nationalists, calling themselves Invincibles, as they walked through the park towards the Viceregal Lodge. Lord Cavendish had been appointed by Gladstone only three days before his arrival in Dublin earlier that day. He and Mr Burke chose unwisely to walk without protection to the official residence in Phoenix Park. As they did so, four men suddenly leapt out and one of them, named Brady, drove a long abattoir knife into the back of Mr Burke, and another, named Kelly, then cut his throat. Lord Cavendish was also stabbed to death as he tried to come to Burke's aid. Both men were then savagely mutilated with surgical knives. Mr Burke had been the principal target of this attack.

He was an Irish Catholic loyal to the Crown's representative at Dublin Castle, and was known as the 'castle rat'.

The Irish Nationalist leader, Charles Stewart Parnell, was accused of implication in the murder, but he had immediately denounced the outrage, saying in his official statement that 'no act has ever been perpetrated in our country during the existing struggles of the past fifty years for social and political rights that has so stained the name of hospitable Ireland as this cowardly and unprovoked assassination of a friendly stranger'. Until the murderers of Lord Frederick Cavendish and Mr Burke were brought to justice, the statement went on, 'that stain will sully our country's name'. It did – English feeling against the Irish was unquestionably hardened by the monstrous act, an example of the entirely unprofitable terrorist assassination. Gladstone offered £10,000 reward for the identification of the killers, and it was made known that any participant in the conspiracy who informed on the others would be immune from prosecution. Long and careful police work eventually led to the arrest of 27 men, three of whom turned informers. Brady, Kelly and three others were sentenced to death and hanged for the crime, and others were given long terms of imprisonment.

President Carnot of France was one of the next important victims of the death-dealers, shot in 1894 by a 22-year-old Italian anarchist named Cesario Santo Hieronimo, who was duly executed by guillotine. A man of proven liberalism and integrity, Sadie Marie François Carnot, the President of the Third Republic, undoubtedly died as a scapegoat for the system. He had just made a speech at a banquet in Lyon, and was on his way to the theatre when he was shot. The assassin was only saved by gendarmes from being violently dealt with by the crowd. The President died four hours later, and his killer was executed. The murder provoked anti-Italian riots in the streets of France. Perhaps national leaders should stay away from theatres. Assassination is a theatrical event in a sense, and assassins may be unconsciously drawn to theatres as the scenes of their performances, for they are usually seeking attention for themselves.

In Bulgaria, Stefan Stambulov, a former teacher, had become chief minister to Ferdinand of Saxe-Coburg, whom he had brought to the throne. Stambulov dealt skilfully and diplomatically with Bulgaria's quarrels with Russia and Turkey, but the cost of maintaining a ready army was met at the expense of the internal economy, and the despotic Stambulov fell from favour, making many enemies. One unsuccessful assassination attempt had been made against him, and the leaders of the conspiracy executed. Stambulov knew perfectly well that he was a marked man, and he claimed to know the identities of those who would be behind the next attempt. 'If I fall,' he said, 'my friends will not desert my wife and the children.'

On 15 July 1895, Stambulov was walking home in Sofia when four men attacked him with knives and guns, and he died from his wounds three days later. Crowds jeered at his funeral cortege, and two of his murderers, arrested only after a year had passed, were given derisory sentences. It was long believed that Ferdinand was implicated in the assassination, but this view is now generally discounted.

Two years later, the Spanish Prime Minister, Antonio Cánovas del Castillo, died at the hands of an anarchist at the baths in Santa Aguada. He was an intellectual, but as leader of the Spanish Conservatives was identified with the policies of the regent, Queen Maria Christina.

In 1898 the President of Guatemala, José Maria Barrios, was shot dead by a rebel against his six-year dictatorship. The Latin American republics were acquiring a taste for assassination which so far has never deserted them. The Dominican Republic, in particular, was to feature largely in the assassination agenda during the twentieth century. In 1898 its President, Ulises Heureaux, was murdered by the leader of an insurrection, Ramon Caceres, whose father had been executed on Heureaux's orders.

Absolute monarchs were still the assassins' favourite targets, though, where they existed, and among them was the Shah of Persia. Nasr-ed-Din had already escaped one attempt on his life in 1852. His succession to the throne as King of Kings was contested by the followers of a Shi'ite mystic, El Bab, whom they believed was the awaited Muslim Messiah, the Mahdi. The Shah had El Bab executed, and many of his followers were massacred. But the sect survived, and the

Babites were the Shah's enemies from then on. It was they who failed in the first attempt on his life, and they who finally succeeded in killing him, in 1896, spurred on by further ruthless suppression after the 1852 attempt. The Shah's murderer was a tradesman from Kerman, scene of the hideous massacre by the Shah Mohammed a century earlier.

The last illustrious victim of an assassin in the nineteenth century was a woman. For obvious reasons we have noticed few attempts on the lives of women hitherto, and those we *have* noticed did not succeed. Perhaps women of power were better protected than their male equivalents, or maybe intending assassins lacked sufficient ruthlessness to murder women in cold blood, for Elizabeth I, Isabella of Spain and Queen Victoria, among others, survived not just one but several plots or isolated attempts against each of them. There were plenty of women of whom one might say that they were more deserving of death than these three, such as Mary Tudor and Catherine de' Medici. But the Empress Elizabeth of Austria became a real victim and an undeserving one.

She was Elizabeth of Wittlesbach, daughter of Duke Max of Bavaria, and in 1854, at the age of sixteen, she was married to the young Emperor Franz Josef. She had been a great catch – a fairytale princess, beautiful and accomplished – and for a time she was a popular empress who brought a touch of class to the Habsburg throne. But the magic did not last. The stifling ritual of the Habsburg court was too much for this passionate free spirit, who loved art and literature, music and riding. She was romantic, and gave money to Richard Wagner. Hating crowds, she preferred to ride across open country, discarding items of clothing for her hard-pressed lady-in-waiting to pick up whilst in hot pursuit. She found her mother-in-law, the Archduchess Sophia, insufferable. Franz Josef's mother had not wanted him to marry Elizabeth in the first place, and now that he had, she was determined to keep her daughter-in-law in line. When Elizabeth was pregnant for the first time, she spent some of her time teaching her pet parrots to talk. Sophia told Franz Josef that his wife ought not to spend so much time with them. 'It can so easily happen.' she wrote, 'that when women look too much at animals in the first months the children come to take after those animals.'

At last Elizabeth could stand it no longer, and she left Vienna. She joined house-parties for the fox-hunting in England and Ireland, and visited the continental spas – anything but return to the Habsburg court. On one occasion Queen Victoria, concerned for her health, lent her the royal yacht for her escapade.

In 1889 Elizabeth's eldest son, the Crown Prince Rudolf, was found dead at Mayerling, near Vienna, with his mistress, the Baroness Vetsera. The details of the tragedy were hushed up. It could have been murder, or assassination, but is now believed to have been a suicide pact. Whatever it was, Rudolf's mother never recovered from the blow, and her health suffered badly. She left Franz Josef to his mistress, the actress Katherina Schratt, and took to wandering about Europe, dressed forever in black. And as she was boarding a steamer at Geneva on 10 September 1898, with Countess Sztaray, her lady-in-waiting, a young Italian anarchist jumped in front of her and stabbed her in the chest with an iron file. She fell to the ground, but then, with a supreme effort of will, the empress, now 60 years old, regained her feet and walked away, saying it was nothing, collapsing only after she had reached the deck of the steamer with the countess's help. Despite her long desertion, the emperor was very distressed by her death.

This was an ignorant crime and ought to be called murder rather than assassination. Elizabeth had no power, yet was killed brutally as a representative of the widely hated Habsburg monarchy which she had herself almost renounced by her actions. The murderer was a callous killer named Luigi Lucheni, a builder's labourer, who seemed proud of what he had done. He had originally come to Geneva with the intention of murdering the Duke of Orleans, but as the duke did not appear he settled for the empress instead. The crime's effect was only to arouse widespread sympathy throughout the empire for old Franz Josef, who declared, 'Nothing has been spared me in this world.' It was all part of the violent madness that was leading inexorably towards the First World War.

6

The Age of Anarchy

The first important victim of assassination in the twentieth century was King Umberto of Italy, who was murdered at Monza on 29 July 1900. His killer was an anarchist named Bresci, who fired three shots with a revolver, though the first was enough to kill the king, the bullet having entered his heart. 'It is nothing,' the king said, as he died. The Mafia was widely suspected of involvement in the murder, but it seems on the evidence that Bresci acted alone, and he was imprisoned for life. Umberto, the son of Victor Emmanuel II, had survived two previous attempts on his life, in Naples in 1878 and Rome in 1897. On the first of these occasions, the king had managed to dodge a dagger thrust at his body by an anarchist cook, Giovanni Passanante, and said, 'These are the risks of the job.' His reign was relatively peaceful, but he was an increasingly absolutist monarch and thus antagonised the left wing in his country.

It was a moot point whether anarchist natives of Italy were more dangerous inside the country or outside it. They had accounted for a French President, a Spanish Prime Minister, and an Empress of Austria before dealing with Umberto, and they were to have an unsuccessful go at King Victor Emmanuel in 1912.

The Italian king was not the first royal target of assassins in the new century, however. That doubtful honour belonged to Edward, Prince of Wales, whilst on his way by train to Copenhagen in April. When the train stopped at Brussels, a fifteen-year-old anarchist named Sipido fired a shot through the prince's carriage window with a revolver. The Belgian stationmaster was the first to grab the assailant, and the 58-year-old prince, soon to become Edward VII on the death of Queen Victoria, kept the badly-aimed bullet as a souvenir.

An attempt was also made on the life of the new Shah of Persia in 1900, during a visit to France. He was riding in an open carriage in the Champs Elysées in Paris when a young carpenter, François Salson, jumped on to the carriage's step and was about to fire a revolver at the Shah when an officer deflected his arm and he was arrested.

In the next year it was the turn of President McKinley of the United States, and it was as if a signal were being given that the country was to rank high among those nations given to assassination and political violence in modern times. It was under William McKinley that the United States first rose to a position of world power, and he was a popular President. On 6 September 1901, he was shot in Buffalo by a man whose hand he was about to shake, at the Pan-American Exposition. The assassin's hand and pistol were wrapped in a handkerchief, and he fired twice at point-blank range, hitting the President in the chest and stomach. As the President's bodyguards jumped on the assailant, Leon Czolgosz, Mr McKinley, all but collapsing with pain, said, 'Be easy with him, boys. Don't let them hurt him.' The President died a week later.

Czolgosz was the 28-year-old son of Polish immigrants, and an anarchist. A conspiracy was immediately suspected, and other anarchists were arrested, but there was no evidence that Czolgosz had not acted alone. 'We open our arms to the human sewage of Europe,' the *Washington Post* complained; 'we offer asylum to the outcasts and malefactors of every nation . . .' And it certainly seems unarguable that wherever Latin peoples, in particular, have gone in the New World – the Spanish and Portuguese to South America; Italians to the United States – they have taken high murder rates and assassination with them. (Although we should not overlook the fact that in Mexico, for instance, which has an unenviable reputation as a country with one of the world's highest murder and assassination rates, the Aztecs already had a bloody tradition of ritual sacrifice long before Cortes and his army turned up there.) But the Polish Czolgosz had shown signs of mental instability for some years, had become an 'anarchist' after reading with fascination newspaper reports of the murder of King Umberto, and had no remorse for his action, which he said was on behalf of the 'good working people' whose enemy McKinley was. The murderer went to the electric chair.

The years from the beginning of the century to the First World War might be called the period of Mediterranean madness. It began with Umberto and continued with Alexander of Serbia. Alexander Obrenovic was a despotic monarch. He had succeeded his abdicated father, King Milan (who had followed the murdered Prince Michael to the throne), when only a boy, and dispensed with liberal constitutional government when he was only seventeen, ruling with a series of puppet governments.

The history of the Serbian monarchy, which was only a hundred years old, was riddled with violence. The Obrenovic and Karageorgevik families had been rivals for the throne since the nation had won its independence from Turkey, and two rulers had already been murdered. In 1817, Kara George (Black George) Petrovic, who had led the first successful Serbian rebellion against the Turks, was assassinated in his sleep, and his head was cut off and sent to Constantinople. The man responsible for this was Milos Obrenovic, and the savage rivalry of these two families culminated in the murder of the last of the Obrenovic rulers, King Alexander.

In 1900 Alexander married Draga Maschin, a widow of doubtful reputation, who had been one of his mother's ladies-in-waiting and was nine years older than Alexander. The marriage aroused great opposition, and in no time all doubts were justified. Queen Draga was acquisitive and ostentatious while the people became poorer and the army went without pay. Anyone who protested was punished. In due course, Draga's brother was named as heir-apparent, and public demonstrations ensued, police opening fire and killing protestors and arresting alleged ringleaders, who included army officers. This was the signal for action. On 11 June 1903, army officers blew open the doors of the royal chamber in the palace at Belgrade. The king and queen were shot dead without ceremony, and their bodies mutilated with sabres before being thrown out of a window to the cry, 'The tyrants are no more!' The queen's brothers and the Prime Minister, as well as some officers loyal to the king, were also killed in a

clean sweep that brought King Peter I of the rival Karageorgevik family to the Serbian throne. He was the grandson of
'Black George', and there is hardly any question as to how far
the Karageorgeviks were involved in the conspiracy.

This assassination was also, however, a sacrifice for the
sake of the people. There was rejoicing in the streets of
Belgrade, where flags were hung out, and King Peter was a
man of courage and integrity who restored constitutional
monarchy to his country. But it seems probable that a satisfactory coup could have been achieved without resorting to
murder. A more interesting question now, however, is how
on earth the deaths of Alexander of Serbia and President
McKinley can be lumped together under one title. There
could scarcely be two more dissimilar killings, and if we
accept the Serbian case as one meriting the word 'assassination', the American one must be counted simply as murder.
It was the deluded act of one man against another, and it
cannot have been conceived by any reasonable human being
as achieving any good, for one President, as a representative
of the individual power which the killer hated, was certain to
be replaced by another. The word 'assassination' elevates the
killing of McKinley into an act of political significance, which
it was not, and the image of the killer into something more
significant than a common murderer – a distinction the
'assassin' usually, if not always, aspires to.

Alfonso XIII, grandfather of the present King of Spain,
survived five attempts to kill him, the first in 1906 when he
was returning from his wedding to Princess Victoria Eugenie
of Battenberg, Edward VII's niece. Dynamite was thrown at
the open coach by an anarchist from a rooftop overlooking
the processional route from Los Geronimos church to the
royal palace in Madrid. The explosion missed its target, but
the new queen's bridal gown was splashed with the blood of
one of the royal bodyguards, and 28 people were killed and
many injured. The killer was named Morales, and he killed
himself before he could be caught. If my memory is accurate, I once saw a veteran motor car with its steering wheel
damaged by bullets in a later unsuccessful attempt on King
Alfonso's life. The growing object of hatred in Spain was not
so much Alfonso as an individual, but more the monarchy as

an institution, and in due course the king was *voted* out of power by the people, and abdicated.

In 1908, King Carlos of Portugal and his eldest son, the Crown Prince Luis, were shot dead in Lisbon by a Republican in an act which inevitably recalls the primitive ritual of sacrifice for the sake of the people. Portugal's troubles at the time were not in any sense the king's fault except that he had appointed the dictatorial Chief Minister who adopted repressive measures to deal with growing discontent. The king himself was a peace-loving man of culture, who translated Shakespeare into Portuguese; but as the figurehead of authority in his country, he was murdered. The killing achieved nothing. The lot of the Portuguese people did not improve under the republic until Salazar became dictator twenty years later, and the cost was that Salazar's rule was to all intents and purposes a return to absolute kingship, since he had all power in his hands and permitted no opposition party.

George I of Greece was the next king to die by violence. The Danish Prince William George of Schleswig-Holstein-Sonderburg-Glucksburg was elected King of the Hellenes in 1863. He was a strictly constitutional monarch, and was well loved by the majority of Greeks. 'My strength,' he said, 'is the love of my people.' But one who did not love him, a Greek named Karditzis, had tried to kill him in 1898. On 18 March 1913, the king visited the new Greek city of Salonika, won when Macedonia was shared out with Serbia after its liberation from the Turks. As he was walking along a street there, he was murdered by a drunken madman, Alexander Skinas. King George had reigned well for half a century.

Meanwhile, the Greek Prime Minister Delyanni had also been murdered in June 1905, and in February 1910, Butrus Pasha Ghali, the Christian Minister of Justice in Egypt, was murdered by a Muslim fanatic, al-Wardani, as a protest against his unpopular internal policies.

Further afield, the Kuang Hsu Emperor of China is reputed to have been killed in 1908 by order of the unscrupulous 83-year-old Dowager Empress Tz'u-Hsi, who had siezed control of the Manchu empire as regent on the elevation of the infant Kuang to the throne. Regicide in China, as in this case and the alleged murder of the Ming emperor in the seventeenth century, was only likely to be committed by members of the imperial family or the court entourage, not so much because the emperor was a sacred figure, but because he was never accessible to the public, living in a closed and heavily guarded palace.

Prince Ito of Japan was killed by a Korean fanatic soon afterwards. Ito Hirobumi was a samurai leader in the revolutionary transformation of Japan, and a liberal statesman who framed the Japanese constitution, being made a prince in 1907. However, his opposition to the Russo-Japanese war led to his disgrace, and having been appointed governor of Korea, which had been made a Japanese protectorate, he was murdered in 1909 during a visit to Manchuria.

In America Presidents Caceres of the Dominican Republic and Madero of Mexico were murdered in 1911 and 1913 respectively. Ramon Caceres had given the Dominican Republic its only period of stable government for many years, and after his death chaos ensued once more. Francisco Madero was a democratic reformer, who was assassinated in February 1913, by agents of General Victoriano Huerta, who siezed power and set the Mexican Revolution in progress.

Between these two, on 14 October 1912, an attempt was made on the life of the former president Theodore Roosevelt of the United States. He was seeking a third term of office, and as he was leaving a hotel in Milwaukee to make an election speech, a man shot him in the chest from two yards away. The bullet had to pass through Roosevelt's metal spectacle case and a thick wad of papers in his pocket. The wounded presidential candidate coughed into his hand, and as there was no blood concluded that the bullet had not pierced his lung, so went ahead with his speech, in a blood-soaked shirt, having intervened on behalf of his would-be murderer who might otherwise have been lynched. The attacker was a German-born bartender named Schrank, who was declared insane and sent to a mental institution for the rest of his life. He believed himself to be the agent of God in preventing Roosevelt from violating the tradition that no president gets a third term. He was also intent on preventing a murderer from becoming president again. It seems he had seen McKinley in a dream, and the ghost had accused Roosevelt of being his assassin. As for 'Teddy', he lived for seven years after the incident with Schrank's bullet still lodged in a rib which it had fractured. It would take more than that to kill *him*, he said.

We should not overlook the more sinister and bizarre aspect of the attempt on Roosevelt – the hint of ritual sacrifice which is also discernible in the assassinations of other modern heads of state. It may be no more than coincidence that the ancient traditions that kings could rule only for eight years, in kingdoms such as Crete, Sparta and Sweden, are emulated by the modern United States, where the same period is the maximum term of office for the country's president; but of course the powerful politician as head of state is nevertheless seen as a king-substitute, and made a scapegoat for the ills of society. One might almost suspect that the insane assassin is more on the wavelength of what Jung called the 'collective unconscious' in this respect than those of us who believe we are guided by logic and common sense.

Back in Europe, events were moving towards a climax, or perhaps to more than one climax. In 1911, Pyotr Stolypin, former Russian Minister of the Interior who had become Tsar Nicholas II's Prime Minister, was murdered in Kiev. The scene of the killing was a gala performance at the Opera House in honour of the royal family – a performance of Rimsky-Korsakov's opera *Tsar Sultan*. When the interval came, Stolypin got up to stretch his legs, turned to the royal box and bowed to the Tsar, and was shot by a smartly dressed young man who had walked calmly down the aisle towards him. The killer was Mordka Bogroff, a Jewish revolutionary who had also become an agent of the secret police, and who had obtained entrance to the carefully guarded theatre with a police ticket. The Tsar made his way immediately to the stage and led the audience in singing the national anthem. Stolypin died five days later. The murderer was hanged. But the question why he did it was never answered, and the motive remains a mystery. Was Bogroff part of a conspiracy, and, if so, who were his fellow-conspirators, or his bosses? Stolypin had been a strong statesman, who had introduced some useful agrarian reforms, but had also prolonged the Tsarist despotism and encouraged the state police to maintain order by terror. Thousands of people were sent to Siberian labour-camps under his ministry. Nevertheless, the expected target of a revolutionary assassin would have been not the Prime Minister but the Tsar.

Jean Jourès of France seemed one of the least likely targets for assassination when he was murdered in a café in the Rue du Croissant in Paris on 31 July 1914. The leader of the French socialists, he had never been in a position of real power. He campaigned for the rights of the individual, founded the newspaper *L'Humanité*, and was a critic of anti-Semitism, becoming one of the champions of Dreyfus in the famous treason scandal. But he was also an opponent of extreme nationalism, and it was a nationalist fanatic who shot him, as the figurehead of the rising tide of socialism which was widely feared and the chief objective of which at the time was peace not war.

The spark that ignited the war in Europe had occurred a month before at Sarajevo. On 28 June the Archduke Franz Ferdinand, Habsburg heir to the Austro-Hungarian throne, and his wife, Sophie von Chotkova, Duchess of Hohenberg, were shot dead in the street by a nineteen-year-old student, Gavrilo Princip. It was yet another personal blow to the aged Emperor Franz Josef, the archduke's uncle.

Franz Ferdinand, son of the emperor's brother the Archduke Charles Louis, had become heir-apparent on the death of Crown Prince Rudolf at Mayerling. No one would have dreamed that he was to become a key figure in the modern history of the world. He was an awkward and sensitive youth, and became mean, impatient and bad-tempered as he grew older. But he was a strong character, and ultimately courageous. The Habsburg court was appalled when it discovered that he was courting, and planned to marry, a lady-in-waiting, the Czech countess Sophie Chotek von Chotkowa und Wognin. Franz Josef told him he must choose between the countess and the crown, but Franz Ferdinand replied that he had to marry Sophie if he was to be any good for anything, and he refused to back down. His obstinacy led to the emperor's reluctant acceptance of a morganatic marriage in 1900. But the affronts to his wife in the Habsburg court, combined with Franz Josef's refusal to take his nephew into his confidence in matters of state, led to Franz Ferdinand's opposition to his uncle's policies.

As Inspector-General of the empire's armed forces, he accepted as a matter of duty the invitation from General Potiorek, the military governor of Serbia, to attend the army manoeuvres in Bosnia, though the dangers were well known. Emigré Serbs in America had called for 'Death to the Habsburg dynasty, eternal remembrance to the heroes who raise their hands against it.'

After the inspection, he was to be welcomed at the town hall of Sarajevo, the Bosnian capital. Franz Ferdinand hated the claustrophobic attention of personal bodyguards, and other security arrangements were practically non-existent. He and his wife were on their way to the town hall in an open carriage when a grenade was thrown. It missed the target and exploded under the car behind, wounding three officers and a number of spectators. The unharmed archduke showed great courage in insisting that his driver stopped while he personally supervised attention to the wounded, and then resumed his programme. The car reached the town hall and the Lord Mayor embarked on the formal address of welcome which the circumstances had now made ridiculous – 'Our hearts are filled with happiness over the most gracious visit. . .' The archduke is said to have remarked sarcastically that the bomb-thrower would 'in true American style, be given a high decoration and perhaps end up as a Privy Councillor'.

The next stage was supposed to be lunch at the governor's residence, but the archduke was concerned about the bomb attack and insisted on first visiting a badly injured officer in hospital – an adjutant, Lieutenant-Colonel von Merizzi. Sophie insisted on accompanying him. On the way there, there was confusion about the route to be taken. The original plan had been changed, for safety's sake, but the archduke's chauffeur had not been given clear instructions. Taking a wrong turn, he was corrected by General Potiorek and, stopping the car, he reversed in order to resume the right route. And all this happened in front of the waiting Gavrilo Princip.

Thomas Becket

Henri IV of France

The murder of the
Princes in the Tower

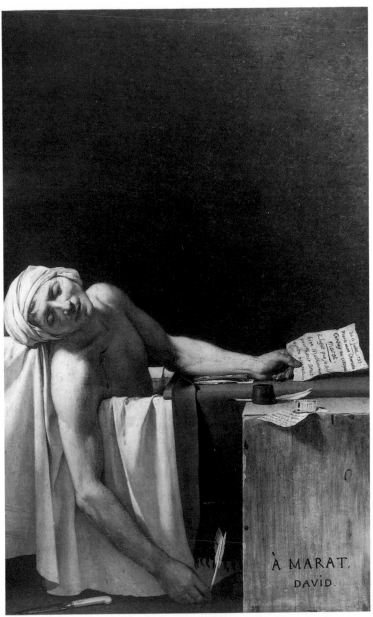

The Death of Marat, Jacques-Louis David's famous painting in the Royal Museum of Arts, Brussels

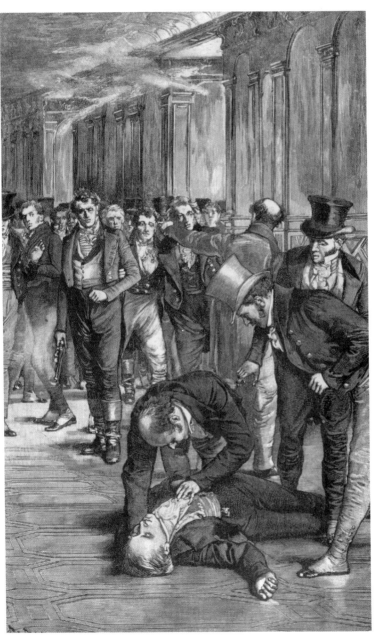

The assassination of Prime Minister Spencer Perceval

Abraham Lincoln

Tsar Alexander II
of Russia

The Empress Elizabeth
of Austria

King Alexander and Queen Draga of Serbia

The Archduke Franz
Ferdinand's tunic after
his assassination in 1914

The 'mad monk' Grigori
Rasputin

Tsar Nicholas II of Russia

Leon Trotsky

John F. Kennedy on the White House steps, a short time before his
assassination in Dallas in 1963

Indira Gandhi with Margaret Thatcher in 1982. One woman survived a later attempt on her life – the other did not

He stepped forward to the car and fired two shots with a Browning revolver. The first bullet hit the duchess, passing through the bodywork of the car and through her corset. The second hit the archduke in the neck and passed through his jugular vein into his spine. 'It is nothing,' he said as his aides rushed to his side, and he managed to gasp, 'Sopherl! Sopherl! Don't die! Keep alive for our children!' But blood spurted from his mouth and both he and his wife were dead within a few minutes.

Princip, who had been seized by people in the crowd and beaten up, having failed in an attempt to shoot himself, maintained at first that he had acted alone, but eventually admitted to a conspiracy. He had not intended to kill the duchess, and regretted doing so, but never showed any remorse for killing the archduke, as a personification of the hated Habsburgs who held the Serbs in subjection. What Princip and his colleagues wanted was the union of Serbs and Croats in an independent nation. What they overlooked in their ignorance was that they were killing the one man who was most likely to meet them halfway, for Franz Ferdinand believed in a federation of states rather than an empire held together by firm central rule from Vienna.

Behind the assassination was a secret nationalistic organisation known as the Black Hand, founded in Belgrade, one of whose high-ranking officers was 'Colonel Apis'. This was the code-name of Colonel Dragutin Dimitrijevic, who had led the assassination of King Alexander and Queen Draga eleven years earlier. Apis supplied Princip and his young friends with bombs and revolvers, and probably financed their attempt to kill the archduke, for they had to travel the 130 miles from Belgrade to Sarajevo and be ready there on the day of Franz Ferdinand's visit. The Austrians thought the Serbian government was the instigator of the plot, and issued an ultimatum which the Serbs could not accept in its entirety. Austria declared war on Serbia a month after the assassination, believing that Russia would not interfere on the Serbs' behalf. But Russia and Germany aligned themselves with the opposing sides and mobilised their forces, and the world war was set in motion.

The disastrous incompetence of the Austrian police and

security service in providing proper protection for the archduke led to suspicions that General Potiorek was implicated
in the conspiracy. It was, after all, he who had invited Franz
Ferdinand to Sarajevo, he who had mishandled the change of
route, and he who had caused the chauffeur to back the car
right in front of Princip.

Disraeli's dictum still held good. The assassination at
Sarajevo was not the *cause* of the First World War. It merely
provided the excuse for the first shots in a situation that was
leading inevitably to war in any case. The Habsburg empire
was brought to an end, and Yugoslavia came into being after
the war.

Princip did not live to see it. Sentenced to twenty years' hard
labour because he was too young for the death penalty, he
contracted tuberculosis in Theresienstadt prison, near
Vienna, lost one of his arms, and died in April 1916. Twenty-
four others stood trial for suspected implication in the assassination. Several of them had taken cyanide after the attack,
which again had been provided for the purpose by Dimitrijevic, but it had failed to kill them. Three older conspirators were hanged, but several, like Princip, were too young
and went to prison. Two others also died there from tuberculosis and malnutrition. Hardly had the assassins' dream of
union between Serbs and Croats been realised than the
Croats began to demand independence from the Serbs.

Princip predicted that he would become a national hero,
and his optimism and the archduke's sarcasm were well
founded. The old Latein Bridge over the River Miljacka in
Sarajevo, near which he had stood when the archduke's car
stopped right in front of him like a gift from the gods, is now
named Princip Bridge, and a nearby building has been turned
into a museum, of which Princip's life and effects are the star
exhibits. Yet to the world at large, it is impossible to think
that, if some modern Dante were to compose a new *Inferno*,
he would not replace Marcus Brutus, as deserving of the
worst torments the imagination can devise, with Gavrilo Princip. 'Our ghosts will walk through Vienna,' he had written on
the wall of his prison cell, 'and roam through the palace,
frightening the lords.'

7

Rendezvous with Death

In the twentieth century, and particularly after the First World War, one might have supposed that political minorities would have recognised the ineffectiveness of assassination as a coercive weapon and that the consequences were too unpredictable to make such killings worthwhile. Events were to prove otherwise.

Russia maintained its well-deserved reputation for domestic assassination even while it was engaged in the war, and among its victims was one of history's most famous and bizarre assassinees. Grigori Rasputin was a Siberian peasant who, calling himself a 'holy man', won the confidence of the Tsarina Alexandra by his apparent ability to help the heir to the throne, Alexis, who suffered from crippling haemophilia. The facts that Rasputin was filthy and smelly, with long greasy hair and beard and black fingernails, that he drank to excess, that he was grossly immoral, all counted for nothing with the empress when measured against his undoubted power to ease her son's pain. Whether by hypnosis or by reducing the boy's emotional stress through suggestion, Rasputin was able to arrest internal bleeding and prolong the life of the young Tsarevitch. The Tsarina believed that he was a saintly miracle-worker who did it by the power of prayer.

Rasputin came to exert an evil influence at the Tsarist court, interfering in politics and military affairs, and adopting such familiar manners with the Empress Alexandra that rumours circulated that she was his mistress, to say nothing of his relationship with her daughters. He was reputed to have raped a nun after failing to seduce her, and he was wont to address ladies of the highest nobility at court as 'my lovely mare'. His real name was Grigori Efinovich – 'Rasputin' was a nickname meaning debauched. His acceptance at court was a national scandal. The Tsar, Nicholas, was uneasy about Rasputin, but typically indecisive because of the monk's beneficial effect on his son and heir and his wife's absolute conviction that Rasputin could actually cure the boy.

It was a group of young officers and noblemen, led by Prince Felix Yussoupov, who took it upon themselves to rid the empire of this lewd and uncouth monk who was even choosing for the Tsar who should run the country, according to whether the men in question approved of Rasputin or not. An attempt to bribe Rasputin into retiring from public life had failed. He must be got rid of by other means.

Prince Yussoupov was one of the richest young men in Europe. His family had been confidants of the Tsars of Russia for generations, and he was heir to his father's vast estates and art treasures. He lived for pleasure, but could see clearly enough that Rasputin was paralysing Russia and destroying the monarchy. His co-conspirators were his friend the Grand Duke Dmitry Pavlovich, the politician V. Purishkevich, Lieutenant Sukhotin, and an army medical officer, Stanislas Lazovert.

A plot was hatched for late December 1916. Rasputin would be invited to a nocturnal party in the cellar of Yussoupov's home, the Moika Palace, whilst the Prince's wife Irina was away at a health resort. The mad monk's favourite cakes and Madeira wine would be laced with cyanide supplied by the doctor. When Rasputin was dead, the others would help to dispose of the corpse. It all appeared very simple.

Prince Yussoupov spent some considerable time cultivating Rasputin's friendship, and then invited him to a midnight supper, using the Princess Irina as bait, for she was a well-known beauty whom the monk had not so far met. Rasputin fell into the trap despite rumours of danger and advice from friends not to go. Arriving at the house, the peasant was taken to the cellar by the prince, who nervously promised that the princess, whom he said was at another party upstairs, would be down shortly.

Rasputin ate two poisoned cakes and drank two glasses of poisoned wine with no apparent ill-effect, and asked Yussoupov to sing to him. He ate more cakes and had his glass refilled several times, but nothing untoward happened. It was not the first time that Rasputin had survived an attempt on his life. A prostitute named Kionia Guseva had been hired by his enemies two years before to kill him in the street, and had plunged a knife into his abdomen, but he had recovered.

After more than two hours in the cellar, Prince Yussoupov went upstairs to consult his panicking colleagues, and came down again with a revolver behind his back. As Rasputin stood looking at a crucifix on the wall, Yussoupov fired at point-blank range, and the monk fell with a scream, and a bullet in his back. The other conspirators now rushed into the room and the doctor, who had said that the poison was enough to kill several men instantly, pronounced Rasputin dead. He was wrong again. The prince, left alone temporarily with the 'corpse', saw the monk's face twitch and his eyes open. Suddenly Rasputin leapt to his feet and, foaming at the mouth, clutched Yussoupov by the throat. The prince managed to free himself and fled up the stairs with Rasputin following him on all fours. Yussoupov yelled a warning to his friends, and while Rasputin tried to escape across the courtyard he was shot again by both Purishkevich and the Grand Duke, and as he fell to the ground the prince beat him about the head frantically until the body lay still in the blood-stained snow. Then it was tied up in a curtain and pushed through a hole in the ice of the frozen River Neva.

Three days later the corpse was recovered from beneath the ice by divers. Rasputin, full of poison and bullets, had amazingly managed to free his arms from the rope that had bound him. He had died by drowning. He was buried in the presence of the Tsar and the imperial family. The conspirators' intention of committing the deed in secret and leaving Rasputin's death a complete mystery had failed utterly, but no one suffered for the killing. It did not achieve its purpose of preserving the monarchy. The revolution soon swept away Tsarist Russia.

Why is the subsequent killing of Tsar Nicholas II in the Russian Revolution nearly always referred to as 'assassination', when the killing of Charles I in the English revolution, and of Louis XVI in the French, are referred to as 'executions'? None of the three deaths achieved any new political end that had not already resulted from the kings' displacements. None of their deaths was necessary to the well-being of the governments which replaced them, except insofar as their continued existence was conceived as a threat to stability and an incitement to counter-revolution. The only difference is that in the case of the Tsar the Bolsheviks shot his wife and family as well in a more extreme case of barbarous slaughter. But as far as the king himself was concerned, this was a case of execution by those who already held power in the state. The Tsar, after all, had been forced to abdicate more than a year before, on 15 March 1917. He and his family had been kept in confinement since then, first at Tsarkoe Selo, then for a few months at Tobolsk, and finally at Ekaterinburg in the Urals. The killing was announced to the general public by a statement after the event, to the effect that the Presidium of the Ural Regional Soviet 'in accordance with the people's will, has decided that the former Tsar, Nicholas Romanov . . . is to be shot'. And so he was, on the night of 16 July 1918. He and his wife, their son and four daughters and several servants were assembled in a small room on the pretence that they were about to be moved yet again. Then a squad of soldiers with revolvers entered and shot them all. The corpses were dismembered and burnt, then finally destroyed with acid, the residue being thrown down a mine shaft.

The death of Nicholas II, like those of Charles I and Louis XVI, was a ritual sacrifice intended to ensure that the revolution which had overthrown him would prosper. Several other members of the Romanov family still in Russia were also murdered separately afterwards.

Lenin, who said that assassination was not a necessary part of revolution, survived an attempt on his own life a month after the Tsar's death, though – ironically enough – it was not carried out by a Tsarist reactionary but by a woman who had long opposed the Tsarist regime. On 30 August, as Lenin was walking to his car after addressing factory workers in Moscow, two women approached him, and one of them drew a revolver and fired three times, hitting Lenin twice, in the neck and shoulder. The woman was Dora Kaplan, and her companion was her sister. Doctors managed to save Lenin, but if the would-be assassin believed that the Bolsheviks were merely replacing one repressive regime with another she was right. Many were executed for alleged complicity in the plot, Dora herself being shot by the commandant of the Kremlin Guard. Fanny, her sister, died in prison many years later.

Although Lenin lived for six more years, his life was shortened by the attempt, for he suffered lung damage. Suspicions have arisen that when Lenin *did* die in 1924, after a series of cerebral strokes, he *was* assassinated. The timing of Lenin's death was fortuitous for Stalin, because Lenin had begun – before the last strokes paralysed him – to undermine Stalin's position as Secretary-General of the Communist Party. Stalin told Trotsky, among others, that Lenin was asking for poison to end his suffering, and after his death, one of his doctors told Trotsky that the medical prognosis had not envisaged Lenin's imminent death. Therefore, Trotsky concluded, Stalin murdered Lenin. There is no proof, one way or the other.

One of Lenin's strongest critics outside Russia was Rosa Luxemburg, one of the leaders of the German communist 'Spartacist' movement. She was a Polish Jew, brought up and educated in Warsaw, but her childhood was attended by physical and emotional suffering due to a congenital hip displacement which, despite long and extensive treatment from the age of five, left her a deformed cripple with a permanent limp. She became involved with socialist revolutionaries in Poland and Switzerland and had begun to get a reputation as a political theorist by the time she moved in 1898 to Germany, where she also became a compelling speaker and a member of the SPD – the Social Democratic Party – later co-founding the German Communist Party (the KPD) with Karl Liebknecht. She denounced the First World War as an imperialist conflict.

On the night of 15 January 1919, after a Spartacist disturbance in Berlin, which she had tried to prevent, had been suppressed by troops, 'Red Rosa', as she was now known, was arrested by armed irregular troops of the Freikorps and taken to the Hotel Eden, where she was identified by an army captain, who then gave instructions for her to be escorted to a waiting car that would take her to prison. But as she reached the street-door of the hotel, she was knocked to the floor by a soldier using his rifle butt, and was carried out and put into the car streaming blood. As the car drove away, an officer shot her in the head, and her body was thrown into the Landwehr Canal. Liebknecht was also murdered. Luxemburg's decomposed corpse was washed up four months later.

The official explanation of Rosa Luxemburg's death, announced the day after the killing, was that she had been murdered and taken away by an angry mob which overpowered her military escort. But the truth eventually came out, and a soldier named Runge was given two years for attempted manslaughter, whilst a Lieutenant Vogel, believed to have shot her, was given a derisory sentence of two years and four months for 'committing a misdemeanour while on guard duty, for illegally disposing of a corpse, and for filing an incorrect report'. Even as recently as 1962, the government of West Germany felt able to refer to the killing as an execution 'in accordance with martial law'. But the killing of Rosa Luxemburg was neither execution nor assassination. It was murder, apparently premeditated.

There was suspicion in some quarters that the death of Lord Kitchener, aboard the cruiser HMS *Hampshire* when it struck a mine and sank on its way to Russia in 1916, was a case of assassination. There had been an earlier German plot to assassinate both Kitchener (the War Minister), and the Foreign Secretary, Lord Grey. The suspicions were fuelled by the Admiralty's refusal to make its report on the incident public. There had been speculation that foreign agents had planted a bomb on the *Hampshire* whilst the ship was being refitted in Belfast; or that spies had betrayed Kitchener's imminent journey to the enemy. In fact, the court of enquiry concluded that the tragedy was an accident, due to ignorance of the presence of a minefield in that area. Of course, courts of enquiry had been wrong before, and would be again.

In 1917 in Britain, a feeble plan was made to assassinate the Prime Minister, Lloyd-George. Three conscientious objectors, Alice Wheeldon, a suffragette from Derby, and her daughter Winnie and son-in-law Alfred Mason, were each sentenced to ten years' penal servitude for conspiring to murder the man they held responsible for the enormous loss of life in the war. They had apparently planned to kill him with curare. The poison, supplied by Mason, who was a chemist, was to be injected either by means of nails in the Prime Minister's shoes, or by pins hidden in his hat, whilst he was playing golf.

The death in 1919 of Emiliano Zapata, the peasant guerilla leader in Mexico, was among a vast number of political killings in the turbulent Latin American republics, and revolutionary Mexico itself was to earn the doubtful distinction of being the world's capital of assassination for a period. Zapata was the epitome of Latin American revolutionaries – generously moustachioed beneath a wide-brimmed hat, armed with sword as well as rifle, and with ammunition belts crossing over his chest. One of his revolutionary maxims was: 'It is better to die on your feet than to live on your knees.' It was to become a favourite saying of Fidel Castro of Cuba in due course.

In 1920 the Mexican President, Venustiano Carranza, was shot dead whilst in captivity, sleeping in a hut which was not properly guarded. Carranza had supported the revolutionary president Madero, and after his assassination, had led the violent opposition to Huerta, who had seized the Presidency. He defeated Huerta and was recognised by the United States as the new President, but was defeated and captured during renewed revolt in 1920, being murdered a few days after his capture.

His death was followed in three years by the assassination of General 'Pancho' Villa, the wealthy rebel and bandit who had formerly been the hero-dictator of northern Mexico and whose return to power – and even popularity – was feared by the government, notwithstanding his appalling record of killing, terror and rape as an outlaw since his displacement. Seven men in the pay of the government and led by a Congressman, Jesus Barrazas, ambushed Francisco Villa while he was driving home in his car with several employees. Bullets rained down on the vehicle killing all the occupants except one, who got away. 'Tell them I said something,' Villa whispered to one of his comrades as he died. Something memorable, he meant, to be invented as famous last words and lend force to his claim to heroism and martyrdom among his supporters. When Villa was already dead, he was shot again in the head at close quarters by Barrazas, who was later photographed with the corpse in a faked impression of state mourning for the former general. Barrazas also went to prison – very briefly – in a pre-arranged pantomine in which he publicly 'took the rap' for the liquidation.

Violence and unrest in Ireland also brought their inevitable assassinations in the early twenties. Field-Marshal Sir Henry Wilson was a distinguished First World War soldier and former Chief of the Imperial General Staff. Now a Member of Parliament, he was also military adviser to the Ulster government, and as he had been born in Ireland, he was seen by the Irish Republican Army as a traitor, organising Ulster resistance to Sinn Fein. After unveiling a war memorial in London in June 1921, Sir Henry was on his way home to 36 Eaton Square. As he alighted from a horse-drawn carriage at his front door, he was shot four times by two men with revolvers. The killers, one of whom had a wooden leg, were caught, but not before they had also wounded two policemen. Reginald Dunne and Joseph O'Sullivan, members of the IRA, were young ex-servicemen. They were duly hanged.

Orders for the killing had been issued by Michael Collins, the Sinn Fein leader and Member of Parliament for South Cork, who had organised the IRA to fight against the British on behalf of a unified republic. Two years earlier, Collins had organised an assassination attempt on the Viceroy, Lord French, but this had gone wrong when his gang of gunmen attacked the wrong car. The killing of Sir Henry Wilson, the first political assassination on English soil since the murder of Spencer Perceval in 1812, provoked civil war in Ireland, and in the following year Collins himself was murdered, having become in the meantime Prime Minister of the newly created Irish Free State. When he signed the treaty of 1921, Collins said prophetically, 'I am signing my death warrant.' He was shot after a gun battle in August 1922, when his car was ambushed whilst he was driving to Cork by extremists who resented his dealings with the British government and Protestant Ulster.

In 1921 Mr Hara, who was stabbed to death in a Tokyo railway station, became the third Prime Minister of Japan to be assassinated in the Taisho Era, between 1912 and 1926, when Japan was emerging as a powerful nation to be reckoned with in world affairs. The previous victims were Count Okuma and Viscount Takahashi. The policy of assassination in Japan was cultivated by the shizoku gentry – the former samurai caste – to force their will on the government. Because it was regarded as a matter of honour in Japanese society, and was not instantly condemned and outlawed, it became all too common. A liberal statesman, Ozaki Yukio, wrote a poem pessimistically embracing his own potential assassins with the lines:

> Praise be to men who may attempt my life
> If their motive is to die for their country.

On the continent of Europe, Walther Rathenau was one of the most significant victims of those years. Rathenau was a wealthy Jewish industrialist and intellectual who became Foreign Minister of the Weimar Republic in 1921. He was a proponent of the welfare state and of European unity. But his liberal policies, and the fact that he was a Jew, both served to alienate German right-wing extremists, who convinced themselves that he was working for communism, Jewish world power, or both, and his assassination was openly advocated.

On 24 June 1922, Rathenau was being driven along Berlin's Königsallee in an open car when another open car with two men in it drew alongside, and one of the men fired several shots at Rathenau at close range. Then the other man threw a grenade into Rathenau's car. The assassins' car disappeared quickly down the street whilst the grenade exploded. A nurse jumped into Rathenau's car to try to help him, but he was dead by the time they got him home.

The men who carried out the murder were named Kern and Fischer. Surrounded later by police, Kern shot Fischer and then himself. But these two were only part of a large conspiracy of extremists who wanted to overthrow the republic and establish a nationalist dictatorship. The familiar bogies of Jews, Marxists, Freemasons, Catholics and so on, as scapegoats for Germany's condition after the war, led to a large number of murders in Germany in these years. Because of the immediate and unforeseen public outcry against the murder and in defence of the democratic principles Rathenau had upheld, nationalist dreams were not immediately realised, but there is no doubt that the death of Walter Rathenau was an important stepping-stone across the tide of German affairs towards Adolf Hitler.

On 10 June 1924, the leader of the socialist opposition in Italy to Benito Mussolini, Giacomo Matteotti, who had made allegations of rigged elections, disappeared in Rome. A few days later his corpse was found in a shallow grave twelve miles outside the city. Two professional gangsters, Amerigo Dumini and Albino Volpi, were subsequently convicted of stabbing Matteotti to death in a car, and Dumini served two years in prison, being paid large sums of money to take the rap and keep quiet. Mussolini denied any knowledge of a plot to kill Matteotti, but Dumini and Volpi had been hired by Mussolini before for acts of violence against anti-fascists, and it emerged that Mussolini had remarked to his staff afterwards, 'If I get away with this we all survive, otherwise we shall all sink together.'

There was strong reaction against Mussolini both in Italy and abroad over the Matteotti affair, and whether the killing was carried out on the dictator's direct orders or on the instructions of fascist extremists without his knowledge, it is probable that his cause would have been done less harm if Matteotti had been left alone.

Mussolini, appointed Prime Minister of Italy by King Victor Emmanuel, survived at least four attempts on his own life in the 1920s. A socialist deputy and war hero named Zaniboni tried to kill him in November 1925, and there were three more attempts in 1926, the last by a sixteen-year-old anarchist named Zamboni. Mussolini adopted on occasions a novel way of protecting himself. When he was travelling by road with motorcycle outriders, he would not be in the official car as expected, but would himself be one of the motorcycle escort.

Mussolini's nonchalant attitude to assassination was presumably formulated on the basis that it is more blessed to give than to receive. 'It is,' he said, 'simply social hygiene – taking individuals out of circulation just as a doctor would take out a bacillus.' He exploited the attempts on his own life to gain sympathy, and for propaganda purposes magnified attacks by isolated assailants into international conspiracies by anti-fascists. It was a trick he taught Hitler.

In the Far East, an attempt was made to take the Emperor Hirohito of Japan out of circulation in 1924, to be followed by a further abortive effort eight years later. Who can say how the premature deaths of the Duce and the Mikado might have affected subsequent history?

In November 1924, Sir Lee Stack Pasha, sirdar of the Egyptian army and Governor-General of the Sudan, was driving through the streets of Cairo on his way home from his office. With him were his chauffeur and an aide-de-camp, Captain Campbell. Suddenly, as the car slowed down at a crossing, several men shot at the car with pistols, and all three occupants were hit, but the chauffeur managed to accelerate and get away. Next day, Sir Lee Stack died from his injuries. Eventually, two brothers named Enayat were arrested and confessed that they were members of a gang, led by Shafik Mansour, which had carried out the assassination. Eight men, including Mansour, were convicted of the murder and sentenced to death, though the sentence of one man was commuted to life imprisonment. Mansour, who was hanged, was a lawyer and Egyptian MP who had been suspected of complicity in the murder of Ghali in 1910.

Mexico was still in the throes of struggle for stability after its period of revolution and anarchy, and in 1928 President Obregon became the latest victim of violence, murdered on the eve of his second term of office by one Leon Toral. Alvaro Obregon had supported Carranza and, as Minister of War, had defeated Villa in 1915, becoming President in succession to Carranza in 1920.

The early 1930s were a bad time for Japanese leaders, too, in the continuing rash of ministerial assassinations, now in the Hirohito era. In November 1930 Prime Minister Yuko Hamaguchi was murdered by a right-wing patriot in a militarist conspiracy. Two years later Prime Minister Inukai Ki was murdered, also by expansionist military factions whose plans he opposed. Nine officers visited his home, and were invited by the premier to discuss their grievances. Their leader, Lieutenant Yamagishi, dismissed the invitation, pointed his pistol at the Prime Minister, and fired, his companions following suit. It seems that the army and navy officers who hatched this plot, and called themselves the Black Dragon Group, also considered the idea of murdering Charlie Chaplin, who was then on a visit to Tokyo, because he was the 'darling of the capitalist class' and his death would precipitate war with the United States. Chaplin was dining with the premier's son when the assassination of Inukai was carried out. The Japanese authorities dealt out lenient sentences to those convicted.

In 1932, President Paul Doumer of France was murdered. On 7 May he was killed by a Russian named Gorgoulov, but this death, so often called assassination, was, like so many others, the murderous act of a madman, and had no political significance. M. Doumer, who was 75, was shot in Paris outside a book exhibition at the Salon Rothschild. He believed a car had hit him, and was not told that he had been shot. His last words were, 'Ah, a road accident. . . '

The attempt on the life of the United States' President-elect, Franklin D. Roosevelt, on 15 February 1933, was likewise without political importance. An Italian immigrant, Guiseppe Zangara, stood on a chair during a speech by Roosevelt at Miami, and fired five shots, none of which hit the target but one of which killed the Mayor of Chicago, Anton Cermak, who was standing beside Roosevelt. This was murder by a lunatic, even though Zangara was judged sane and electrocuted. Apparently he held capitalists responsible for his chronic stomach pains, and he shot at Roosevelt simply because he was rich and powerful, having previously thought of killing the King of Italy and President Hoover for the same reason.

This, at any rate, was the official interpretation of the event. But it seems to be a distinct possibility that this so-called attempt on the life of the President-elect was a deliberate red herring in what was in reality the well-organised assassination of Mayor Cermak. For Anton Cermak had embarked on a mission to 'wipe out the Mafia' in Chicago, and his murder may have been instigated by Al Capone.

Cermak himself believed that he was a victim of Mob violence, and it turned out later that, so far from being crippled with stomach pains, Zangara was a fit man and an experienced marksman. Furthermore, Cermak had been standing some distance from Roosevelt at the time he was shot.

The King of Afghanistan, Mohammed Nadir Khan, was assassinated in November of the same year. The former general had been recognised as king of his country by the British in an effort to bring stability to the independent buffer state between the Soviet Union and British India. It had been torn by rebellion and seemed under threat from Russia. But Nadir instituted westernising reforms which aroused the anger of the Muslim clergy, and he was duly eliminated.

8

War Crimes

The peak year for assassination in Europe was 1934, heralding the move towards the Second World War. In July, Dr Engelbert Dollfuss, Chancellor of the Austrian republic, was shot dead in the Chancellery in Vienna. His murderers were Austrian Nazis trying to stage a *coup d'état*, which failed. The diminutive Dr Dollfuss had tried to escape when the Nazis had seized the Chancellery, and although they had orders to avoid bloodshed the Chancellor was shot by a warrant officer, Otto Planetta, and died from his wounds through neglect, no one bothering to get him to a doctor. International denunciation of the failed attempt to take over the country forced the Nazis to disown the whole business, and Planetta and several others were hanged, while hundreds of their supporters were imprisoned.

Adolf Hitler was attending a performance of Wagner's *Rheingold* at Bayreuth when he was given the news of the killing. He could scarcely disguise his delight, but took trouble to behave normally after the opera. 'I must go for an hour and show myself,' he said, 'or people will think I had something to do with this.'

Later that year King Alexander of Yugoslavia, grandson of Alexander of Serbia, made an official visit to France. He was met at Marseilles by the Foreign Minister, Jean Louis Barthou, and as they were driven away from the harbour, immediately after the king's disembarkation, a man jumped on to the running-board of the car and shot both the king and M. Barthou. The king died almost at once, M. Barthou an hour later, through loss of blood, after wandering unrecognised among the crowd, in a semi-coma, apparently searching for his spectacles. The assassin, Vlada Chernozamsky, was a Croat member of an extreme terrorist group, the Internal

Macedonian Revolutionary Organisation. He was shot dead by a French officer. But Chernozamsky was working for another extreme group, Ustase, on this occasion, and was in the employ of the latter's notorious leader, Ante Pavelic. Pavelic was in Italy, whence the money and passports of the conspirators had come, when he was sentenced to death in France, but Mussolini refused to extradite him, and Pavelic was subsequently responsible for the deaths of many thousands of Serbs.

It is probable that only the authoritarian king was the target and that M. Barthou was shot by accident. Barthou, who was in his seventies, was a cultured Frenchman, an author and music-lover who possessed a fine library. It is also possible that the killing of both men was instigated by Hitler or, perhaps more probably, by Mussolini, who had long supported Croatian extremists. From Italy's point of view the disintegration of Yugoslavia resulting in a separate Croat nation under Italian patronage would form a useful buffer to German influence in the Balkans. Hitler was the chief immediate beneficiary of the killings, however, for Barthou had been firm in withstanding Nazi demands and had been active in strengthening French alliances with eastern Europe.

Mystery also surrounded the killing of S. M. Kirov in Leningrad on 1 December 1934. Sergei Kirov was chairman of the Leningrad Soviet and a member of the Politburo. He was second only to Stalin in the Bolshevik hierarchy, and widely venerated and honoured in the Soviet Union, many places and organisations being named or re-named after him, the best known of which was Leningrad's former Mariinsky Ballet Company. He was shot dead in a corridor outside his office in the heavily guarded former Smolny Institute by a young epileptic cripple, Leonid Nikolayev, who then fainted and fell beside his victim. He subsequently tried to cut his own throat, but survived and was interrogated under torture, where he stuck rigidly to his claim that he had acted alone. One story put out was that Nikolayev had killed Kirov because he had caught him in bed with his wife. All the evidence points to Stalin's guilt, however, and Kruschev later hinted at it. Kirov's bodyguard had been withdrawn a few days earlier on the instructions of the NKVD, and it was never satisfactorily explained how the assassin had managed to get past the security guards in the Communist Party headquarters. Nikolayev was full of paranoid resentment. He was a communist who had been dismissed from various posts as being untrustworthy. Kirov's death was followed by the Stalinist purges and terror of the next few years, and it seems fairly certain that the murder was engineered by Stalin, via his secret police, as an excuse for the repressive measures which followed. Two of those condemned were Kamenev and Zinoviev, who had made up the quadripartite leadership with Stalin and Trotsky after Lenin's death. Zinoviev was accused of moral complicity in Kirov's murder and of being involved in a plot against Stalin's life. Trotsky's end came later, in 1940.

In 1936, yet another Japanese government minister, Admiral Saito, fell victim to an assassination squad armed with swords and sub-machine-guns in an attempted coup, the chief object of which was to murder and replace Emperor Hirohito. This time, the law came down heavily on the rebels, thirteen of whom were executed.

A half-hearted attempt was made in that year on the life of Edward VIII by a man named George McMahon. As the king was riding on horseback along Constitution Hill on his way to Buckingham Palace, McMahon aimed a revolver at him and was about to fire when a special constable knocked the firearm out of his hand. McMahon claimed that a foreign power had paid him £150 to kill the king. This unlikely story aroused the suspicion that McMahon was out of his mind, but he was given a year's imprisonment with hard labour, and by the time he was freed Edward VIII had abdicated.

Three years later, shortly before war was declared, an Australian in London, Vincent Lawlor, was packed off to his native country after he had been convicted of firing a shot with a sawn-off rifle at Princess Marina, the Duchess of Kent, in Belgrave Square. The man was mentally unbalanced. The day before, he had fired a shot through the window of the Earl of Harewood's London home.

There were some grounds for suspicion about the death of Pope Pius XI in 1939. The pope died after being injected with a stimulant by Dr Francesco Petacci, his personal physician.

Dr Petacci's daughter Claretta was Mussolini's mistress, and Mussolini had remarked in 1938 that he was hoping for the pope's death 'very soon'. The Duce described the papacy, significantly, as a 'malignant tumour in the body of Italy', that must be 'rooted out once and for all'. The pope had been on the point of denouncing fascism. His successor, Pius XII, was much criticised for his failure to attack fascism, to say nothing of Hitler's treatment of the Jews, strongly enough.

In March 1940 Sir Michael O'Dwyer, who had been governor of the Punjab when the notorious Amritsar Massacre had occurred, in 1919, was shot dead in London. Sir Michael had given his official approval to the suppression of the riots, and defended the officer who had so ruthlessly exceeded his duty, General Dyer. There had been strong agitation in India for O'Dwyer's impeachment, but nothing had come of it. Now 75 years old, Sir Michael was attending a lecture at Caxton Hall, and was on the platform with several other former Indian civil servants and the Secretary of State for India, Lord Zetland. When the speeches had ended, a Sikh walked to the front of the platform and emptied a revolver at the group of men. Two bullets hit Sir Michael, one passing through a kidney, the other through his heart and right lung. Three other men were wounded. The Sikh was immediately overpowered. He was Singh Azad, a 37-year-old engineer. Tried for murder, Singh, whose English was poor, showed no remorse for what he had done and denied that he had any accomplices. In his diary were two notes of Sir Michael's name, one of them spelt 'O'Dyer'. It seems likely that Singh, who was hanged, had mistaken his victim for General Dyer.

Despite being the founder, with Lenin, of the USSR, and creator of the Red Army, Leon Trotsky's opposition to Stalinist policy got him expelled from the Communist Party in 1927. He and his family were exiled at first to Alma Ata, near the Chinese border, and deported from Russia altogether two years later. He had become a thorn in Stalin's side and had to be removed, like the others. Trotsky continued his revolutionary work, first in Turkey, then in France and Norway, but always harassed by Stalin's agents, and he was eventually sentenced to death, *in absentia*. Stalin had removed all opposition to his personal dictatorship except Trotsky, the most

103

influential of all his opponents. Having made the mistake of exiling Trotsky rather than having him killed earlier, Stalin now feared that his old rival would become the focus of a concerted effort to displace him.

In 1937, Trotsky moved to Mexico with his wife, where they built a veritable fortress at Coyocáu, with high concrete enclosure walls, and the revolutionary theorist continued to write widely-read and influential attacks on the regime of the man who had unexpectedly beaten Trotsky in the contest for the succession to Lenin. Stalin ordered Beria, his chief of secret police (the NKVD) to have Trotsky killed by any means. One man chosen to do the job was a fanatical Spanish communist, Ramon del Rio Mercador, who evidently planned his task with great skill and patience.

He began by seducing an American girl communist on holiday in Paris. She was Sylvia Ageloff, and she was carefully chosen because she had two sisters, Hilda and Ruth, who worked for Trotsky in Mexico City. Having ostensibly fallen in love with Sylvia, Mercador said he would join her in America, which he duly did, and then prevailed on her to go to Mexico with him and introduce him to her sisters and, of course, to Trotsky.

Meanwhile, Beria's alternative plan had been tried and failed. An assault party of about twenty men had been let into Trotsky's house by a traitor, and they had burst into Trotsky's bedroom and riddled the sleeping figure under the covers with sub-machine-gun bullets and quickly made their escape, after cutting telephone and alarm wires and throwing a few incendiary bombs for good measure. But Trotsky was not under the covers. Well aware that he was a marked man, and ever alert to danger, he had heard an unusual scuffle downstairs, and had stuffed bedding under the blanket and hidden in a wardrobe. When Mercador – now calling himself Frank Jacson – appeared on the scene, Trotsky was busy reinforcing the house's defences.

Mercador patiently worked at gaining Trotsky's trust by posing as a journalist disciple who could be useful to him in his work. At length, on 20th August 1940, the assassin approached Trotsky in his garden and asked him to look at an article he had written. The two men went indoors to Trotsky's study, and while the 61-year-old revolutionary sat reading at his desk, the 26-year-old Mercador stood behind him, drew a mountaineer's ice-axe from beneath the trench-coat he had kept over his arm, and brought the steel head crashing down on Trotsky's skull.

Trotsky screamed out and managed to rise from his chair, grasp at Mercador and bite his hand before his wife and aides rushed in. The guards would have killed Mercador instantly if the blood-drenched Trotsky had not forbidden it, for he wanted the man to talk. Rushed to hospital, Trotsky, who believed he had been shot, was operated on immediately, but the blow had caused massive brain damage and he died the following day.

Mercador served nearly twenty years in prison in Mexico, during which he was made a Hero of the Soviet Union in his absence. It is said that he feared, on the one hand, reprisals from Trotskyists, and on the other, death from Stalin's agents so that he would not talk. He never did, though at one point he tried to make out that, as a Trotskyite, he had only turned against his leader when he was ordered to go to Moscow and assassinate Stalin. On his release, he went first to Cuba, courtesy of Fidel Castro, then to Czechoslovakia, apparently settling in Prague.

This is the generally accepted version of Trotsky's assassination. Much doubt has been thrown on it over the years, not least because of the almost incredible choice of Mercador as hit-man for such an important mission. He was a bundle of contradictions, and when he killed Trotsky he was armed with a loaded revolver, yet chose to hit him with a weapon which did not kill him at once, saying afterwards: 'I took it in my fist and, closing my eyes, I gave him a tremendous blow on the head.' Stalin's hired assassin had to *close his eyes* to carry out his task? Well, truth is often hard to swallow, and in the absence of plausible alternatives this is the story we are left with. Trotsky's eldest son had died in suspicious circumstances, and Trotsky had at one time contemplated suicide in Mexico, thinking that his death would satisfy Stalin and perhaps obtain the release of his youngest son from prison in the Soviet Union. Mercador's weird mother, Caridad, also stalks through the shadows of these events like an *éminence grise*, but it is hard to believe that she was the real instigator of the murder, as has been suggested.

Perhaps the best-known assassination of the war years was that of Reichsprotektor Heydrich in Prague in 1942. Reinhard Heydrich, Himmler's SS second-in-command and one of the ghastliest of Hitler's evil lieutenants, well named the 'bloody butcher' and 'hangman Heydrich' in countries under Nazi occupation, was appointed by Hitler in September 1941 as Reichsprotektor of Czechoslovakia. Members of the Czech underground movement plotted to remove this monster from their midst, in an operation code-named 'Anthropoid', and on 26 May 1942 Heydrich was mortally wounded by a bomb as his car was ambushed in the streets. The attack was carried out by two Free Czech sergeants, Jan Kubis and Josef Gabchik, who had been parachuted into the country by the RAF.

The killing of Heydrich as an act of tyrranicide was without question justifiable, taken on its own; but whether the operation was well-advised in the circumstances is another matter. It was planned in London to forestall any possible alliance between Czechoslovakia and Nazi Germany arising out of Heydrich's alluring promises to those who cooperated and his hideous threats to those who did not. But the people in London did not have to suffer the consequences of the Reichsprotektor's murder. Those who did were the people of Lidice, where the assassins were alleged to have come from, and many other victims of Nazi reprisals, mostly Jews.

On 11 June, a chilling German radio announcement from Prague said that because the inhabitants of Lidice had given support and assistance 'to the murderers of SS Obergruppenfuehrer Heydrich, the male adults have been shot, the women have been sent to concentration camps and the children have been handed over to the appropriate education authorities. The buildings of the locality have been levelled to the ground, and the name of the community has been obliterated.' In fact, it seems that 172 men and youths and 7 women were rounded up and shot; 195 women and 90 children were sent to Ravensbrueck concentration camp. Many other children were taken to Prague for examination by 'racial experts' to see if they were fit for re-education as Germans. Those who were not were put in the gas chambers at Treblinka. The village of Lidice, a few miles west of Prague, was burnt, demolished and erased from the face of the earth, and the nearby village of Lezaky was similarly wiped out.

In Prague, meanwhile, the assassins had joined other members of the Czech resistance in hiding in the crypt of a church. Eventually they were betrayed by one of their own number, Karel Curda. German troops arrived on the scene and killed three men with machine-gun fire, but failing to flush out the others with tear-gas, they flooded the crypt. The remaining conspirators shot themselves with their last bullets. Curda, the traitor, was executed by the Czechs after the war.

Was all this loss of life worth the satisfaction of eliminating one Nazi savage among so many? It is a question only the Czech people of the time were entitled to answer. This case was certainly a contradiction of the defence of assassination on the grounds that the death of one man saves the suffering of many. The beneficial effects of the assassination tended to be exaggerated by those who masterminded it. It was claimed, for instance, that it had impeded the German war effort, when in fact it was no more than a propaganda victory for the Czechs and even that was achieved more by the Nazi reprisals than by the murder itself. One would have thought, perhaps, that the instigators in London – Eduard Benes and the exiled Czech government – might have heeded the cases of Marat and others which ought long ago to have established what we may term the Third Law of Assassination: the killing of a person who is in the vanguard of a movement greater and more powerful than the individual victim will be accompanied by the most savage reprisals against the innocent as well as the guilty. Hitler invoked our second law as well. 'If the Czechs do not like Heydrich,' he said, 'I will send them someone worse.'

Admiral Jean Louis Darlan, the chief minister of Vichy France during the period of increasing collaboration with Hitler's Germany, was shot dead in Algiers on Christmas Eve, 1942, by a young royalist and Gaullist fanatic, Fernand Bonnier de la Chapelle, who – like many others – saw Darlan as a traitor, although the admiral had been brought round by this time to cooperating with the Allies. 'If I could meet Darlan,' Churchill had said to Eisenhower, 'much as I hate him, I would cheerfully crawl on my hands and knees for a mile if by doing so I could get him to bring that fleet of his into the circle of the Allied forces.' Darlan's murder definitely served Allied purposes, since there had been a lot of hostile reaction to his appointment as an Allied naval commander. Churchill wrote: 'Darlan's murder, however criminal, relieved the Allies of their embarrassment in working with him, and at the same time left them with all the advantages he had been able to bestow . . .' Nevertheless, Darlan's assassin was tried by court-martial and, after denying that he had any accomplices, he was shot by a French firing squad two days after the murder. Some thought the British had put him up to the job. It could just as easily have been the Americans or the Free French.

There were, of course, a great many killings in Europe during the Second World War that might technically be labelled assassinations but which were really acts of war in exceptional circumstances. There were also one or two deaths that are sometimes referred to as assassinations but which remain unproven. One of the latter was the death of King Boris III of Bulgaria in August 1943. Boris had declined to ally himself with Hitler in the Fuehrer's Russian campaign, although he had declared war on Britain and the United States to oblige the Axis powers. Three days after a meeting between the king and Hitler, during which Boris refused to change his policy, the 49-year-old monarch died suddenly. Rumours that he had been poisoned spread rapidly, but evidence of foul play has never been produced.

It has not been proven, either, in the case of General Sikorski, who was allegedly assassinated in the same year. Wladislaw Sikorski was the leader of the Polish government-in-exile in London and commander of the Free Polish army which was fighting on the side of the Allies. In April 1943, the Nazi Propaganda Minister, Josef Goebbels, announced the discovery in Katyn Forest of the mass graves of thousands of Polish officers slaughtered by the Russians in 1940. Sikorski called for an investigation by the International Red Cross, and Stalin angrily broke off diplomatic relations with his Polish allies, accusing Sikorski of complicity with Hitler. The Russians alleged that it was the Germans themselves who had perpetrated what was to become known as the Katyn Massacre.

Some weeks later, in July, General Sikorski was aboard an aircraft which took off from Gibralter carrying him, his daughter and a number of other passengers back to Britain after a morale-boosting visit by Sikorski to his troops in the Mediterranean. Seconds after take-off the aircraft crashed into the sea, and the Czech pilot, Captain Prchal, was the only survivor. Goebbels immediately announced that the British had sabotaged the plane because Sikorski had become an embarrassment in their relations with the Russians. An official enquiry, supported by the pilot's own testimony, concluded that the crash was an accident, due to a technical failure. But doubts continue. Few people are persuaded that Churchill ordered the assassination of Sikorski, despite the efforts of the German playwright Rolf Hochhuth. But could the crash have been another of Stalin's sinister doings? On 13 April 1990 (Good Friday), the USSR finally admitted its guilt in the Katyn Massacre, which was carried out by Stalin's NKVD. The truth about Sikorski's death remains hidden.

Only a few weeks earlier, the Americans, with President Roosevelt's blessing, had shot down an aircraft carrying Admiral Isoruku Yamamoto, the mastermind behind the Japanese attack on Pearl Harbor and commander-in-chief of the imperial navy. United States intelligence had decoded radio messages about the admiral's movements, and his plane was destroyed with no survivors. Hitler may have tried a similar tactic against Winston Churchill. On 1 June 1943, an aircraft took off from Lisbon on its way to London. Nazi intelligence knew that a British VIP was on board, and may have thought it was Churchill. The plane was shot down by the Luftwaffe over the Bay of Biscay, but the VIP was not the Prime Minister; it was the actor Leslie Howard, returning home from a lecture he had delivered in Madrid on behalf of the British Council.

The assassination occurred in 1944, in Cairo, of Lord Moyne, by Eliahu Ben Zouri and Eliahu Hakim, two young

Jewish terrorists. They had earlier taken part in abortive attempts to kill Sir Harold MacMichael, the High Commissioner in Palestine. The assassins acted on behalf of Lohmey Heruth Israel – Fighters for the Freedom of Israel. Lord Moyne was the British Minister for the Middle East, and was chosen as a representative of the government which had refused immigration to the future Israel of thousands of Jews fleeing from Hitler's Europe. On one occasion Moyne is said to have been offered, by a German agent, a million Jewish lives in return for 10,000 lorries, and to have replied, 'What would I do with a million Jews?' Hakim shot Lord Moyne three times in his official car on the drive of the Minister's Residence. Ben Zouri also shot and killed Lord Moyne's chauffeur, Lance Corporal Fuller, when he tried to intervene. The two men pleaded guilty to killing Lord Moyne without revealing any of their accomplices, and were hanged. The killing was a stupid and futile gesture.

The one assassination of the 1930s and 1940s that most probably would *not* have been futile, but which never took place, was the killing of Adolf Hitler. There were several plots by high-ranking army officers to depose Hitler by *coups d'état*, but these came to nothing, and the actual and apparent attempts at assassination failed. The world needed at this time a military officer with access to Hitler who was prepared to sacrifice his own life in the interests of humanity. Two or three such men duly appeared.

The first alleged attempt occurred in Munich in November 1939. Hitler addressed his party cronies at the Bürgerbraükeller, as he did every year on the anniversary of the so-called Beer Hall Putsch of 1923. A few minutes after Hitler had left, a bomb exploded behind the stage. Seven people were killed and more than 60 injured. The British were promptly blamed for the attack, and two British intelligence officers were kidnapped in Holland and held responsible, being sent without trial to a concentration camp. But the truth of the matter appears to be that this 'plot' was a hoax, hatched by the Gestapo to increase both Hitler's popularity and hatred of the British among the German people. It turned out that a German carpenter and electrician, Georg Elser, had planted the time-bomb in a pillar at the beer-hall, with a mechanism which allowed it to be detonated from outside. Elser, a communist, had been taken by the Gestapo from Dachau and promised his freedom if he would cooperate in this plan. Of course he never *was* freed, being murdered before the end of the war. There is some doubt as to whether Hitler was in on the plot or not. He is reported to have said afterwards: 'Now I am content! The fact that I left the Bürger-bräu earlier than usual is a corroboration of Providence's intention to allow me to reach my goal.'

Other *genuine* attempts on Hitler's life were badly planned or incompetently carried out – bombs failed to detonate, etc. – or were foiled by the Fuehrer's deliberate last-minute changes of plan. Aware of the danger, he said, 'The only preventive measure one can take is to live irregularly – to walk, to drive and to travel at irregular times and unexpectedly.' High-ranking German officers had long plotted to overthrow the Fuehrer to save Germany from the further consequences of his folly. Colonel von Gersdorff and Captain von dem Bussche volunteered at different times in 1943 to commit suicide in order to kill Hitler by deto-nating bombs in their greatcoat pockets whilst standing close to the Fuehrer. Both attempts had to be aborted because of Hitler's sudden changes in his plans.

The most famous and serious attempt by Germans to kill Hitler, albeit too late to save the world from his madness, came in July 1944. The man of the moment was Colonel Klaus Philip Schenk, Count von Stauffenberg. He was a courageous soldier who had fought in the desert campaign in North Africa and been seriously wounded when his car had driven into a minefield. He had lost his left eye, his right hand, and two fingers of his other hand, as well as sustaining other injuries. Long before this, he had become one of the anti-Nazi conspi-rators. Gaining promotion to a post that gave him regular access to the Fuehrer, Stauffenberg took on the responsibility of killing him, after elaborate plans had been made by his colleagues to take over the state immediately on Hitler's death. Part of the original plan was to kill Goering and Himmler at the same time, but this over-ambitious idea led to two lost opportunities to dispose of Hitler, and finally Stauf-fenberg decided to deal with Hitler alone.

On 20 July, Stauffenberg flew from Berlin to Rastenburg to answer a summons from Hitler to make a report on the organisation of the Army Reserve, of which Stauffenberg was Chief of Staff. The colonel carried a briefcase containing official papers, a clean shirt, and a time-bomb. He was accompanied by an adjutant, Lieutenant von Haeften, who also had a bomb in his briefcase – a reserve in case the first should fail. On arrival at the heavily armed and strongly defended Wolfsschanze ('wolf's lair') where Hitler then had his headquarters, Stauffenberg immediately learned of the customary change in Hitler's plans. The conference scheduled for one o'clock had been brought forward half an hour because Mussolini was due to arrive later. It was to be held in a former wooden barrack hut, the walls of which had been reinforced with concrete. Field-Marshal Keitel hurried Stauffenberg from his office to this location, but the colonel, on the pretence of having forgotten something, quickly went back, opened his briefcase and set the bomb to go off in ten minutes.

Hitler was standing at one side of a long wooden table looking at maps, with others all round him. He glanced up as Keitel entered with Stauffenberg. The colonel stood a few feet to Hitler's right and put his briefcase on the floor, two yards from the Fuehrer's feet. As the minutes ticked by, Stauffenberg left the room on pretence of taking an urgent telephone call. Then another officer found Stauffenberg's briefcase in the way of his feet, and moved it to the other side of one of the table's heavy supports. At eighteen minutes to one the bomb exploded.

The walls and roof were blown out, bodies and debris flew in all directions, and fire broke out. Stauffenberg, in no doubt that everyone had been killed, made his escape with Haeften, flying back to Berlin, where the senior officers of the conspiracy prepared to carry out a coup. But Hitler was not dead. His life had been saved by the shifting of the briefcase, the solid table-support protecting him from the worst effects of the blast. His legs were burnt, his back injured, his right arm temporarily paralysed, and his ear-drums punctured. He staggered to the door with his hair smouldering, his face black and his trousers in shreds, but indubitably alive.

The Fuehrer revenged himself on the conspirators without mercy. 'They must be hanged like cattle,' he said, after declaring in a radio broadcast, with megalomaniac effrontery, that the attempt on his life was a crime 'unparalleled in German history'. Stauffenberg and Haeften had already been executed by firing squad. Many senior officers were hanged slowly from meat-hooks with piano wire, and their death agonies filmed so that Hitler could see their suffering at his leisure. Rommel, who had been in on the plot to depose Hitler but had objected to assassination on the grounds that it would make a martyr of him, was permitted to commit suicide. Some of the generals on the eastern front who were in on the plot, and had been issued with phials of poison in case they fell into the hands of the Russians, swallowed them instead to avoid falling into the hands of Hitler. It is believed that seven thousand men were arrested, and nearly five thousand of them executed.

It had all been too late, in any case, to change history. The unbelievable and almost ludicrous repeated failure of all the attempts to assassinate one of the most evil monsters in the history of the human race ended in February 1945, when Albert Speer, Hitler's Armaments Minister, apparently hatched a wondrous scheme to introduce poison gas into the ventilation system of the Fuehrer's underground bunker, but abandoned the idea for technical reasons. Why, for God's sake, one inevitably wonders, did not *someone* simply walk up to the maniac with a revolver, as so many assassins have done over the centuries, and shoot him dead on the spot? The question, alas, has no satisfactory answer. It was left to Hitler to do the job himself, when it was all far too late.

9

The Hired Assassin's Trade

Soon after the war had ended in Asia, the young King of Siam (renamed Thailand by this time) was killed. In June 1946, Ananda Mahidol, the twenty-year-old king, was found in his bedroom at the Barompinan Palace in Bangkok, after a single shot had been heard. The king had a single bullet wound in his forehead. At first his death was reported as suicide or the result of an accident with his own revolver, but no one really believed these stories. The body had been discovered by a page, Nai Chit, who had run through the palace shouting 'The king's shot himself!' Rumour of assassination spread quickly through Bangkok and the chief suspect was the premier, Pridi Banomyong, who had been involved in a conspiracy to overthrow the monarchy in the early 1930s and had been exiled for some years. Investigation soon discounted accident or suicide, and at length the page, Nai Chit, another page, Butr, and a former private secretary of the king, named Chaleo, were charged with conspiring to kill the monarch.

Meanwhile a *coup d'état* occurred, led by Marshal Pibul Songram, who had been involved with Pridi in the conspiracy of 1932. Investigation into the king's death dragged on and, when at last the trial of the three suspects was held, it was delayed again by an abortive attempt by Pridi to regain power. The trial did not end until 1951, five years after the death of King Ananda VII. It confirmed that the king had been murdered, but concluded that the cases against Chaleo and Butr were not proven. Moreover, it was said that Nai Chit could not have fired the fatal shot, though he was guilty of involvement in the conspiracy. The Appeal Court and the Supreme Court then overturned the acquittals of Chaleo and Butr, and all three men were executed. Whoever was really behind the king's assassination, it is generally accepted that

there was a conspiracy to overthrow the last Oriental monarchy and open the way for a communist take-over. If so, it
was a conspicuous failure.

In 1948, also in Asia, the first assassination occurred which
made a deep impression on me, then a teenager, and gave me
a lasting interest in what I saw then, and still see to a large
extent, as the terrible and awesome assumption every
assassin makes – that he is entitled to make a God-like judgement. The murder in question was that of Mohandas Gandhi,
the father of modern India – that 'man of straw', as Churchill
called him, who would 'be forgotten in a few years' time'. It
seemed obvious even then that Gandhi would be remem-
bered for at least as long as Churchill himself.

On 30 January 1948, four days after the first anniversary of
India's independence, Gandhi walked across the lawn of the
house in Delhi where he was staying, to attend an open-air
prayer meeting. Crowds surged around him as he walked
between two young women who supported the frail 78-year-
old Mahatma, just recovering from one of the fasts that had
brought him close to death. One young man stepped forward
into Gandhi's path and raised his joined hands in Hindu
greeting. Gandhi responded in like manner. Then the man
pulled a revolver from his clothing and fired three times,
hitting Gandhi in the abdomen, chest and groin. '*He Ram, He
Ram* (Oh God, Oh God),' Gandhi gasped as he fell, joining
his hands in a gesture of prayer. Within half an hour the man
Indians called Bapu (Father) was dead. Prime Minister
Nehru broke down and wept when he was told. I well remember his moving radio broadcast: 'The light has gone out of our
lives and there is darkness everywhere . . .'

The first automatic reaction to the news, on the part of the
Hindu majority, was that the Mahatma had been murdered
by a Muslim. Lord Mountbatten, the Governor-General of
India, turned on a man who shouted out that a Muslim had
done it and retorted that it was a Hindu, even before he knew
the facts. It was a quick-thinking precaution, and it was as
well that he was proved right. The assassin was a Brahman
newspaper editor from Poona, Nathuram Vinayak Godse.
He had to be rescued by police from the shocked and outraged crowd and from an Indian Air Force sergeant who

proposed to shoot him on the spot. Godse denied at first that he was part of a conspiracy, saying that he had killed Gandhi for agreeing to the partition of India which gave away part of the country to the Muslims. He was outraged by Gandhi's expressions of sympathy for Muslims subjected to Hindu violence in Delhi. The existence of a plot was well known to the police, however, and protection for Gandhi had been advised and offered, but the Mahatma refused it. At length the truth came out. Godse and a schoolmaster, Narayan Apte, were hanged, and several other Hindu extremists involved in the conspiracy, including Godse's brother, were imprisoned. It was a relief that the conspirators were Hindus and not Muslims, for it is terrible to contemplate the slaughter that might have occurred in India if a Muslim had killed Gandhi. Even so, many other Hindu fanatics were assaulted, and one killed, in revenge attacks. 'Cut me in little pieces,' said the chillingly unrepetent Godse, 'and I will still maintain I did right.'

In fact, it may be that, by his death, Gandhi achieved part of the good end that he had struggled to achieve while he was alive, for his assassination shocked a great many in both India and Pakistan into the realisation that the murder was symbolic of the chaos that was threatening the Indian subcontinent.

I am not aware that any serious attempt was made on the life of Jawaharlal Nehru, but he was, of course, as all such powerful men must be, fully conscious of the possibility. On at least one occasion he confused his bodyguards by ordering his driver to go *behind* a dense crowd lined up to see him, and explained to them afterwards that any assassin present would have been at the front.

In September of the same year as Gandhi's death, Count Folke Bernadotte, a Swedish nobleman who had been active in rescuing Jews from their inevitable fate in Nazi Germany, was murdered in Jerusalem, by Jews. Count Bernadotte was a close relation to the Swedish royal family, and had spent much of his life in good works, with such organisations as the Red Cross and the Boy Scouts. As well as his work for refugees in the war, he acted as a go-between when Himmler tried to negotiate a German surrender with Eisenhower without Hitler's knowledge. In 1948 the count became a United Nations mediator between Arabs and Jews in Palestine. He felt it his duty to attempt the task of bringing lasting peace but, not surprisingly, was pessimistic about his chances of success. He did succeed in arranging a temporary truce, but proposed a partition on new lines which Jewish fanatics considered favourable to the Arabs.

On 28 September, Count Bernadotte was in a United Nations car in Jerusalem, with a driver and two colleagues, when the car was stopped by soldiers in a jeep. One soldier ran over to the car and opened fire with a sub-machine-gun, killing Count Bernadotte and one of his companions, Colonel Serot. The perpetrators of this outrageous and completely futile killing were thought to be members of the same Stern Gang of extremists which was believed responsible for the death of Lord Moyne in Cairo.

In the same month, in Argentina, a plot was uncovered to assassinate the President, Juan Domingo Perón, and his wife, Maria Eva Duarte. The plan was to throw a bomb as the Peróns arrived at the Teatro Colon Opera House in Buenos Aires for a gala performance. Thirteen alleged plotters were arrested – a motley bunch which included two women, three priests and a doctor who was almost blind. Their leader was apparently Cipriano Reyes, leader of the meat packers' union, who had been instrumental in Perón's return to power after the United States-inspired attempt to overthrow him in 1945. He was tortured in prison, and an American embassy official, John Griffiths, who had been ordered out of the country for anti-Perón activities, was also accused of involvement.

In response to a speech from Perón denouncing the traitors, the crowds yelled 'Hang them! Hang them!' The beloved Evita (who had once advised a government deputy '. . . if you hear anyone speak ill of me, break his head open') wondered why anyone would want to kill a 'humble woman'.

Before coming to a crop of Middle East assassinations of the 1950s, we might note briefly one attempted and one alleged assassination affecting what were by this time recognised as the world's 'Great Powers'. In 1950, two Puerto Ricans attempted to kill President Truman in Washington.

Truman was living in a temporary residence whilst the White House was undergoing redecoration, and on 1 November the two men, Collazo and Torresola, tried to storm the building, Blair House, but never got anywhere near the President. A brief gun battle ended with the killing of Torresola and a policeman, and the wounding of Collazo and two other police officers. The would-be assassins' aim, apparently, was to draw attention to the cause of Puerto Rican independence. The attempt to kill Truman, like the murder of Count Bernadotte, was conceived in ignorance, for Truman had in fact actively supported the very cause Collazo claimed to be working for. He was sentenced to death in the electric chair, but Truman commuted the sentence to life imprisonment.

In 1953, Joseph Stalin died in Moscow, or possibly at Kuntsevo, just outside the city, where he had his country retreat. According to the first official announcement, he suffered a stroke in his Moscow apartment a few days before his death. If that were true, why had he been moved from central Moscow, with its up-to-date medical facilities, to Kuntsevo, which is where he was seen on his deathbed by his daughter Svetlana? According to the death certificate, Stalin died of a cerebral haemorrhage, but suspicions that he might have been murdered have never been allayed, and the certain facts never clearly established.

Stalin was by then alcoholic and increasingly unstable. Suspicion falls most easily on L. P. Beria, the boss of the NKVD, who had motive and opportunity to poison Stalin, whom he evidently planned to succeed, although Stalin had nominated Malenkov. Two of the bodyguards responsible for Stalin's safety on his deathbed committed suicide after his death. Later that same year Beria was shot as a traitor, according to official announcements, though it is believed he may have been executed much sooner after Stalin's death. Khruschev revealed – or at any rate alleged – that Beria had 'spewed hatred' at the paralysed and unconscious Stalin as he watched at the dictator's deathbed, then fell on his knees when the dying man briefly recovered consciousness. There were various discrepancies in the official accounts of Stalin's collapse and death. It is of no great consequence, perhaps.

All that matters is that the life of the bloody tyrant who had ordered the deaths of so many came to its own overdue end.

The 1950s saw the last violent deaths of kings. The decline of regicide is due largely, of course, to the fact that monarchy itself is on the wane, and those kings who were still left were mostly constitutional monarchs with relatively little personal power. Mere figureheads were becoming less attractive as targets for assassination, except by lunatics, as political causes took over the imaginations of those with a taste for violent action in making their presence felt. In the Middle East, however, there still existed monarchs with real power, and it was there that regicide had its last fling.

An attempt had been made by communists to kill the Shah of Persia in 1949. The incident occurred whilst the Shah was visiting the University of Tehran to celebrate the anniversary of its foundation. He was walking from his car towards the Faculty of Law building when four shots were fired from among a group of newspapermen and photographers nearby. Three of the bullets passed through the Shah's military cap without touching him, but the fourth hit him in the face near the cheekbone and came out under his nose. The Shah's officers and retinue, police, public and photographers scattered in all directions, and the Shah was left standing, with blood pouring down his face and uniform, facing his assailant, who was about to fire again. Unable to run for cover or duck, the Shah dodged about so that he was not an easy target. The fifth bullet hit him in the shoulder and the sixth stuck in the gunman's revolver. The man then threw the gun down and tried to escape, but he was killed by the Shah's officers.

An Iranian Prime Minister, Ali Razmara, was assassinated in March 1951, during the unrest caused by the radical speeches of Mohammed Mussadeq, the demagogue Prime Minister subsequently arrested and imprisoned by the Shah for unconstitutional behaviour. Razmara was killed by members of the Islamic Fedayeen, which was modelled on the original Assassins of Hassan ibn-al-Sabbah. They had also murdered a former premier, Abdul-Hussein Hazhir, and the Education Minister Ahmad Zangeneh. The murderer of Razmara, one Kalil Tahamsebi, was automatically sentenced to death, but the sentence was later quashed and the murderer was praised as a 'soldier of Islam'.

Then King Abdullah of Jordan was killed. Abdullah Ibn Hussein had been one of the leaders of the Arab Revolt against Turkey in the First World War, with 'Lawrence of Arabia', and became sovereign of the Hashemite kingdom of Jordan in 1949. The king was a moderate voice in the hysterical dispute over Israel, and aroused Egyptian and Palestinian resentment. He was shot by a young Palestinian in July 1951, as he entered the Mosque of Omar in Jerusalem, in the presence of his grandson, Hussein, who came to the throne a year later, after the brief reign of Abdullah's mentally unstable son Tallal ended with his abdication. Hussein was to be the target of many assassination attempts.

Seven years after Abdullah's death, Abdullah's nephew, King Feisal II of Iraq, was murdered, together with his family. A military coup was responsible for this act. When the royal palace was attacked by General Kassem, the king surrendered it with the promise of safe conduct for his family, but when he and the queen and their children were in the courtyard, soldiers opened fire with machine-guns and killed the last two young princesses with their bayonets. The mutilated bodies were then dragged through the streets of Baghdad, along with that of the Prime Minister, Nuri as-Said, who had been caught trying to escape disguised as a woman.

This ghastly deed was encouraged by Colonel Nasser of Egypt, who made speeches openly calling on Jordanians to kill King Hussein, too, since Feisal and Hussein, cousins, had formed an alliance between Iraq and Jordan as a counterbalance to Nasser's Egyptian alliance with Syria which was known as the United Arab Republic. But Nasser himself was the target of several unsuccessful assassination attempts between 1954 and 1966, one of which, according to *Spycatcher* author Peter Wright, was engineered at the time of the Suez crisis in 1956 by MI6 and bungled. King Saud of Saudi Arabia was alleged to have spent more than a million pounds in abortive attempts to have Nasser killed, and the CIA were also allegedly involved in a plot to kill him, at the request of Prime Minister Anthony Eden and with the approval of President Eisenhower. An agent is said to have been despatched to Cairo with poisoned cigarettes for Nasser, but failed to go through with the plan.

In 1956, the year before the Suez crisis occurred, British newspapers were preoccupied with the mysterious disappearance of a Royal Navy frogman, Commander 'Buster' Crabbe. The disappearance occurred during the visit to Britain of the Russian premier, Bulganin, and the Party Secretary, Khruschev, on the battleship *Ordzhonikidze*, which docked at Portsmouth. Eventually a headless corpse was washed up there and identified as Crabbe's. It seems that MI6 had engaged Crabbe to go down and measure the propellor of the Russian battleship on behalf of the Royal Navy, which was very curious about it, but a security leak had forewarned the KGB of the spying expedition.

Nikita Khruschev escaped assassination in 1958. It was he who had ordered the ruthless suppression of the Hungarian uprising in 1956. In April 1958 Khruschev visited Hungary, going to Budapest and then on to the mining town of Tatabanya, a few miles to the west, where the youths of the town planned to assassinate the Soviet leader in revenge for their murdered relatives and friends. But the 25 young conspirators were found out through their inexperience and, though they never got a chance to fire a shot at Khruschev, their blood was added to that of the earlier Hungarian rebels.

In other troubled parts of the world, failed assassination attempts included those on Sukarno in Indonesia, Nkrumah in Ghana and Bourguiba in Tunisia. We may never know whether the suspicious aeroplane crash in Africa in 1961, in which Dag Hammarskjoeld, Secretary-General of the United Nations, died, was an assassination or not. He was very unpopular in some quarters, especially Russia, and despite all official assertions that the crash was an accident doubts remain.

As for the death of Patrice Lumumba, often referred to as assassination, that was arguably a case of execution, and, if not that, then murder, although it seems that the CIA was implicated in a plan to assassinate the former Prime Minister with poison. The plot apparently had the backing of Eisenhower, for Lumumba was seeking Russian aid in the Congo crisis and, according to United States fears, turning the country into another Cuba. But Lumumba met his death from within the Congo before those outside could get at him.

Anastasio Somoza Garcia, head of the rich Somoza family that ruled Nicaragua, was murdered in 1956 after twenty years as President of the republic, during which his personal rule became very unpopular because of his despotism and violation of human rights. But his killer was a mentally unbalanced young man – backed by opponents of Somoza's dictatorship, to be sure, but without any real political motive except to kill the hated man. Nothing changed, Somoza's sons took over the country, and the conspirators were all executed or imprisoned.

The case of Solomon Bandaraneike in 1959 was similar. Prime Minister of Ceylon since 1956, he had aroused fierce opposition on the question of Ceylon's official language, hotly disputed between the speakers of Sinhalese and the speakers of Tamil. Bandaraneike had come to power by championing the Sinhalese cause under the banner of the Sri Lanka Freedom Party, and much rioting followed his attempts to establish Sinhalese rather than English as the island's official language. In September 1959, two Buddhist monks visited him at his home and one of them shot him with a revolver hidden in his robe, the Prime Minister dying next day. Nothing changed. Solomon's wife, Sirimavo, succeeded him, becoming the world's first female Prime Minister, and she persisted in making Sinhalese the only official language whilst establishing Ceylon as the republic of Sri Lanka. The Tamil separatist movement still brings strife to that small country today.

Stefan Bandera was a Ukrainian émigré living in Munich, from where he led agitation for the independence of the Ukraine from the USSR. In 1959 he was murdered outside the door of his apartment by a KGB agent, Bogdan Stashinsky, who fired a cyanide capsule in his face. It was suspected locally, at first, that the Americans were responsible for the killing, though why that should be so is not easy to imagine. Two years later, however, Stashinsky defected to the west, and told the full story himself – an unwilling assassin, according to his own account.

Right across the world in the Dominican Republic, the assassination of the President became the most sensational public death of 1961. Rafael Leonidas Trujillo y Molina had, since 1930, been an absolute dictator of the worst kind. His rule was cruel and senseless; his weapons corruption and terrorism. His so-called 'public works' were mainly to the advantage of himself and his family, and he re-named the capital, formerly Santo Domingo, 'Trujillo City', though the old name, given it by Christopher Columbus, has now happily been restored. He gave himself a megalomaniac string of titles, from Generalissimo and 'El Jefe' (The Chief) to 'Liberator' and 'Benefactor'. Hostility to Trujillo grew quickly during the fifties, particularly after his attempt to have President Betancourt of Venezuela assassinated. As a result of this, in 1960, all Latin American countries cut off diplomatic relations with the republic, which had also provided sanctuary for deposed dictators such as Perón of Argentina and Batista of Cuba. The United States imposed sanctions and a ban on arms sales.

On 30 May 1961, Trujillo's car was ambushed on a lonely road near the capital by a group of men headed by an army officer, and Trujillo was machine-gunned to death. Although nearly all the assassins were tortured and executed, their action achieved long-overdue reform in the Dominican Republic, for Trujillo's family was expelled and the regime destroyed. Allegations were made eventually, and not strenuously denied, that the American CIA was behind this assassination, as well as Somoza and other South American dictators who were not the United States' best friends. The guns used to mow down Trujillo were supplied by the CIA.

The chief target of assassins during the early 1960s, however, though none of them ever succeeded, was General Charles de Gaulle. From 1961 to 1965, seventeen assassination attempts on the French President are recorded, and in the 21 years from 1944 to 1966 he was the target of no fewer than 31 plots in all – a world record for a head of state, although some were murder attempts by isolated individuals and not all the plots hatched led to actual attempts. The first occurred at Dakar when a solitary gunman, who regarded de Gaulle as a traitor to France, prepared to shoot him from an escort vessel as the general stood on the bridge of a cruiser sailing into the port. But the would-be assassin was interrupted at the critical moment, while de Gaulle stood to attention during the playing of the 'Marseillaise'.

Most of the attempts on de Gaulle's life came after he had come out of retirement to resume power as head of state in 1958 and were perpetrated by the terrorist OAS (Organisation de l'Armée Secrète) headed by General Raoul Salan. This group was opposed to de Gaulle's Algerian policy, and some of their attempts were extremely well planned and organised, though they all failed and some had to be aborted. They tried to kill him with bombs, grenades and dynamite, machine-guns, high-powered rifles and revolvers, booby-trapped dogs and cyanide pellets fired from a camera, but de Gaulle seemed, like his old enemy Adolf Hitler, to be immune. One man named Bernard committed suicide after failing to get near enough to de Gaulle to shoot him with a revolver. Another plan was to plant a bomb in the President's box at the Comédie Française, but this idea was never put into practice.

Like Julius Caesar, whom he resembled in some respects, Charles de Gaulle should have heeded the warnings and kept a careful watch for his enemies, as John Masefield put it in *The Rider at the Gate*:

> Beware of the Court, of the palace stair,
> Of the downcast friend who speaks so fair,
> Keep from the Senate, for Death is going
> On many men's feet to meet you there.

But all de Gaulle would say to those who worried about his safety was, 'I am doing my job. You do yours. De Gaulle is not going to be kept in a glass case.'

The most elaborate attempt on de Gaulle's life occurred on 22 August 1962, when a team headed by Lieutenant-Colonel Jean-Marie Bastien-Thiry, who had masterminded several previous attempts and was known to his colleagues as 'Germain' or 'Didier', attempted to ambush the general's car whilst he was on his way, with his wife, from the Elysée Palace to Villacoublay airport. This attempt was given the code-name 'Operation Charlotte Corday'. Men with machine-guns were supposed to bring the Presidential car to a halt at a certain point in the Avenue Petit-Clamart, by bursting its tyres, then take care of the outriders and entourage whilst other marksmen shot de Gaulle. But the whole plot came to grief because the first machine-gunner hesitated when given the signal to fire. The signal was too distant for him to see it clearly and unmistakably. When the shooting started, the general's chauffeur accelerated and outwitted a car which chased it at 75 miles an hour through the streets of Paris. A hundred and fifty shots were fired altogether, hitting buildings, shops and a café as well as the Presidential car and an outrider's motorcycle, but neither President nor Mme de Gaulle, nor the adjutant and driver in the car, were hit. De Gaulle's chauffeur in the Avenue Petit-Clamart had perhaps learned something useful from Napoleon's coachman in the Rue Saint-Nicaise.

The café Le Trianon which had been hit by the assassins' bullets was subsequently renamed Le Trianon de la Fusillade. Fifteen men were identified as the assassination squad, and of those brought to trial most were sentenced to life imprisonment. Bastien-Thiry was sentenced to death, along with Alain Bougrenay de la Tocnaye and Jacques Prévost, but in the event only Bastien-Thiry was executed – shot by firing squad.

Other attempts to eliminate de Gaulle followed. No failed assassination attempt from 1963 onward, however, could compete in the world's consciousness with the one against another head of state across the Atlantic Ocean which succeeded in November of that year, and which has unquestionably become one of the most famous and notorious assassinations in the history of the modern world.

10

The American Way of Death

So many volumes have been written about the killing of President John F. Kennedy in Dallas on 22 November 1963, that it would be futile to detail here all the arguments, disputed 'facts', doubts and speculations that remain widespread after nearly 30 years. The Kennedy killing is the best-documented assassination of all time, although I must make the point that if the report of the Warren Commission is accepted as it stands, and Lee Harvey Oswald *was* the sole killer, acting entirely alone, then Kennedy was not assassinated at all – he was murdered.

All the questions that are still being asked seem to add up to a desperate yearning to show that this murder *was* assassination; as if death of this President, mourned perhaps by more people throughout the world than any other murdered head of state, might possibly be less harrowing were it seen to be the work of a rational, political conspiracy rather than the insane act of a single psychopath. Young as he seemed, Kennedy was widely accepted as a father-figure – a king-substitute, perhaps, from whom the people derived their strength and purpose – and they were devastated by his death. For this reason my proposal that Kennedy's death should be classified as murder, at least until proof of conspiracy is produced, will never be generally acceptable, because mere murder in public appears to belittle a national event of major significance. Nevertheless, there has been a growing tendency in recent years for writers, impatient after a quarter century of seemingly unprofitable speculation, to pour scorn on the conspiracy theory as the pet hobby of assassination buffs.

We should not forget those 80-odd threatening letters in Abraham Lincoln's drawer in the White House. They were par for the course for a United States President's term of office, and still come in at the rate of hundreds every year, mostly from cranks but all demanding serious investigation by the secret service. No man who lived in constant fear of being shot at would volunteer for the job of President of the United States, and JFK used to joke about it sometimes. For example, when a motorist speeded past the Presidential car once, Kennedy said to his friend and travelling companion Charles Bartlett, 'They shouldn't allow that. He could have shot you, Charlie.'

At the end of 1960 one such man got through the net and nearly killed Kennedy before he even became President. His name was Richard Pavlick. He was known to Senator Kennedy's security men as someone who had made threats, but they did not know that he was outside the Kennedy mansion on the morning of Sunday, 11 December 1960, with seven sticks of dynamite strapped to his body. He was waiting for the President-elect to go to church. When Kennedy's car came out on to the road he planned to crash his own car into it and detonate the explosives, killing himself as well as the Senator. What stopped him was the appearance of Jacqueline Kennedy and her children. He had no wish to kill them and decided to wait for another opportunity, but before this happened he was tracked down by the secret service and jailed. He was a lunatic from New Hampshire who had fixed his sights on the notoriously corrupt leader of the Teamsters trade union, Jimmy Hoffa, at first, and then decided to have a go at the new President instead.

There is a strong instinctive resistance in most people to accept a simple explanation when faced with the death of a major political figure, and the sudden and unexpected deaths of eminent men have frequently led to suspicions of foul play. Americans still speculate about who might have been involved in the Lincoln assassination and was never found out; and they also felt a similar need to unearth a conspiracy when McKinley was shot in 1901, as if, by discovering enemies on whom they might vent their grief or vengeance, they would be better able to lay the ghosts that haunt them.

Nevertheless, it is certainly true that there are too many unanswered questions about the Kennedy killing for comfort, and the loudest early protests at the Warren Commission's conclusions came from outside the United States rather than from within – chiefly from Britain and Europe. To remind readers briefly of what happened, President and Mrs Kennedy were riding with Governor Connally and his wife through Dallas in a motorcade when the President was shot in the head and neck with a high-powered rifle, and died before he reached hospital. Governor Connally was shot and wounded. One or more shots were identified as coming from the sixth floor of the Texas School Book Depository building as the President's car passed it, and Lee Harvey Oswald, who worked and had been seen there, was arrested an hour and twenty minutes later, by which time he had shot and killed a police officer who had tried to detain him. Two days later, Oswald was himself shot dead by a local night club owner, Jack Ruby, as he (Oswald) was being transferred from the Dallas city gaol to the county gaol. President Kennedy's successor, Lyndon Johnson, appointed a commission to enquire into the assassination, headed by Chief Justice Earl Warren. It concluded that Oswald was the sole assassin, acting entirely alone, and that there was no evidence whatever to suggest that there had been a conspiracy to assassinate the President.

There were immediate doubts in a great many minds about this conclusion. The direction and number of shots fired was one of the major points of dispute. Not the least of the mysteries was why Jack Ruby shot Oswald and the implications of this event for the conspiracy theory; for the claim that he did it to save the Kennedy family the ordeal of Oswald's trial was certainly the most unbelievable thing in the entire business. Ruby was a night-club and strip-joint operator involved in organised crime and illicit gambling in Dallas, who supplied prostitutes and free booze to local police officers and could rely on them to turn a blind eye to his activities in return for his favours, and was hardly the kind of character to put his own life at risk out of tender feelings for Mrs Kennedy, and he confessed later that he had made up his story.

After the barrage of criticism of the Warren Report's 'lone assassin' conclusion, few people remained really convinced that Oswald, who had no reputation as a crack marksman and no apparent personal motive for wanting to kill the President, had acted without a single accomplice, and speculation ran

THE AMERICAN WAY OF DEATH

riot. Among the first theories were that the CIA or the KGB had done it. Moscow was considerably embarrassed when it heard of the killing, because of Oswald's known connection with the KGB (he had been to Moscow in an attempt to defect to the Soviet Union but had been rejected). The USSR may have sent a disinformation agent, posing as a defector, to allay any possible United States suspicions that the Soviet Union was implicated in the murder. As for the CIA, its relations with Kennedy were very strained because of his refusal to provide air cover during the Bay of Pigs fiasco, which had been planned under Eisenhower and had included CIA promises to the Cuban exiles that such air cover would be forthcoming. However, neither of these theories has been shown to have much substance.

Kennedy's dubious policies towards Cuba's communist leader, Fidel Castro, though, do feature strongly as a possible motive in the conspiracy theories. Kennedy had said to *New York Times* reporter Tad Szulc, ten months after his inauguration, 'What would you think if I ordered Castro to be assassinated?' When Szulc replied that he did not think the United States ought to be a party to murder and political assassination, Kennedy said, 'I agree with you completely,' and added that he was under pressure from advisers to give the go-ahead for an attempt but was resisting.

There were those who had wanted Johnson in the White House, as a tough Texan who would understand the strong anti-Castro sentiment in the southern states. But even Johnson was startled to find, when he took office, that 'we had been operating a damned Murder Incorporated in the Caribbean', and attempts to have Castro murdered only ended with Kennedy's own death.

Plots against the Cuban leader began with Eisenhower, who gave his approval to CIA plans, one of which was to assassinate not only Fidel Castro but also his brother Raul and Ernesto 'Che' Guevara. And plans to eliminate Castro continued throughout Kennedy's presidency, whether he resisted them or not. All sorts of wild and wonderful schemes were dreamed up, until the missile crisis of October 1962 caused a pause in the CIA's anti-Castro activities, but they were then resumed up to the time of Kennedy's death.

The CIA was involved in at least six plots to assassinate Castro between March 1961 and March 1963. The first two plans involved feeding Castro with poison pills. One such attempt had been made whilst he was on a visit to the United Nations in New York and probably had the support of President Eisenhower as well as that of Secretary of State John Foster Dulles. Of the other efforts, one came near to success when a cafeteria employee was persuaded to put a cyanide pill into the Cuban President's regular milkshake. When the time came, however, the refrigerated capsule was frozen and brittle, and broke before it could be put in the drink. Subsequent CIA plots involved firearms and explosives. Other attempts were certainly made on Castro's life, with the participation of Cuban exiles in the United States, and some would-be assassins were executed. One CIA-backed assassination team was picked up in Havana a year before President Kennedy was shot, and another abortive plot against the Cuban President was instituted by the deposed dictator Batista, who was himself the intended victim of a plot. The plot against Batista did not, apparently, have Castro's backing, he having gone on record as opposing political assassination as a useless exercise. Yet when he said at a press conference in June 1963 that American agents were meeting with terrorists to assassinate Cuban leaders, he added that Cuba would 'answer in kind'.

It is difficult to ignore the sinister fact that the one thing that Oswald and Ruby had in common was a connection with Cuba. Oswald had been active in pro-Castro propaganda in New Orleans, and was connected later with anti-Castro Cubans, whilst Ruby had been involved in gun-running to Cuba, had business links with Havana, and was linked with the Mafia's anti-Castro efforts later. Lyndon Johnson was reported before his death to believe that Oswald had acted either under the orders or the influence of Fidel Castro. But it is equally plausible that the assassination was a retaliation by anti-Castro Cubans who bitterly resented the reduction of United States support for Castro's overthrow after the Cuban missile crisis of October 1962. Kennedy averted the very real danger of nuclear war at that time, by giving his assurance to the USSR that there would be no United States invasion of Cuba provided the Russians withdrew their nuclear installations. When this had been done, he withdrew support from the anti-Castro Cubans in the United States so that there was no possibility of the USSR accusing the Americans of going back on their promise and renewing the danger of a Third World War.

The CIA had conspired with United States crime syndicates to eliminate Dr Castro to their mutual advantage. A Mafia boss, John Roselli, was alleged to have been the middle-man between the CIA and the hit-men in Havana, where drug-trafficking and illegal gambling had been flourishing under the Batista regime. Castro had driven organised crime out of Cuba, and a Chicago hoodlum, Sam Giancana, was apparently offering $150,000 in 1962 to hire hit-men to kill Castro. Attorney General Robert Kennedy was very angry when he was informed about the CIA's alliance with the Mafia, because he had a mission to crush organised crime in the United States, and one theory is that President Kennedy was killed because of his brother's efforts to convict Teamsters union boss Jimmy Hoffa of criminal activities. Hoffa was known to have made a threat against the Attorney General and may have been persuaded that a strike against Jack Kennedy would be more effective than one against Robert.

Another theory to have emerged is that Kennedy was killed because of his campaign against the Mafia bosses, who thought they had bought immunity by helping the CIA in anti-Castro efforts. When Johnny Roselli later hinted that Ruby's killing of Oswald was *also* a conspiracy, and said that Ruby was 'one of our boys', he opened his mouth once too often. His dismembered corpse was found in an oil drum floating in the sea off Florida. The Kennedy crusade against organised crime died with the President.

The more time goes by, of course, the less likely becomes any certainty of proving without question exactly what happened on that fatal day of 22 November 1963. The Warren Commission was not told by the CIA about its various plots against Castro, and it was not told by the FBI about Oswald's known contacts with anti-Castro Cubans. These facts were among those which led to the setting up by Congress in 1976 of a House of Representatives Select

Committee on Assassinations, which finally turned the tide in official attitudes towards the assassination of John F. Kennedy by concluding that the President was 'probably assasinated as a result of a conspiracy'. It also concluded that two gunmen had fired at the President; that the Warren Commission had suppressed vital evidence; and that the Mob had 'motive, means and opportunity' for the killing.

Perhaps the worst *result* of the Kennedy murder was that it appeared to trigger a new explosion of political violence in the United States and possibly elsewhere. The bullet was seen shattering the President's head over and over again on television, in the now-famous amateur film made by the spectator Abraham Zapruder: as was the murder two days later of Oswald by Ruby whilst Oswald was in the custody of Dallas police. The blaze of publicity that surrounded the event and its aftermath made Oswald as world-famous as his victim, and undoubtedly stimulated fantasies and imitative ambitions in mentally-disturbed individuals. After Kennedy's death, an adolescent boy 'gave himself up' to the FBI, 'confessing' that he had paid Oswald to do the job.

The death of Kennedy heralded a five-year period in which the Americas were to be the focus of the most notorious assassinations of the sixties. Only one public murder in that decade – that of Dr Hendrik Verwoerd in South Africa – would rival in world coverage and sensationalism the events in America in the mid-sixties. Even the murder, three weeks before that of Kennedy, of Ngo Dinh Diem in South Vietnam, seems to have been largely an American affair.

Diem had become President of the new South Vietnam Republic in 1955, under United States patronage, being a Roman Catholic, American-educated anti-communist. But he established a repressive regime, with his brother Ngo Dinh Nhu as head of the secret police and other members of his family in key offices, and antagonised the country's Buddhists. The Americans became nervous of the consequences, threatening first to withdraw their support for President Diem if he did not sack his brother and then cautiously backing a plan through the CIA for a military coup in the country if Diem failed to end repression. The Vietnam generals staged their coup on 1 November 1963. At first the President and his brother refused to surrender, but in the early hours of the following morning they were arrested in a Catholic church. They were put into an armoured vehicle with their hands tied behind their backs, and the major in charge of the operation then stabbed Nhu with his bayonet and shot them both with his revolver.

The shocked United States government declared that it was no part of its policy to have Diem and his brother murdered, but its indecisive attitude towards Diem was a disaster. It resulted in the removal of a mandarin and opened the way to successive military coups and increasing instability in Saigon. President Kennedy said that Diem had spent nine years fighting the communists and deserved better than assassination. Before the month was out, Kennedy himself was dead, and he deserved better, too. Kennedy had intended to withdraw some United States troops from Vietnam after Diem's overthrow, but this policy was reversed within days of Kennedy's assassination and United States involvement in Vietnam was escalated by Lyndon Johnson.

In 1965 a secret Islamic court in Iran issued a death sentence on the Prime Minister, Hasan-Ali Mansur, who was the Shah's man and had been responsible for exiling the mullah Ayatollah Khomeini, who was a thorn in the side of the Shah and his government. The Ayatollah, when told of the sentence, gave his tacit approval. A few days later, Mansur was shot in Teheran's Baharestan Square. Three bullets hit him, in the throat and stomach, and he died six days later. The assassin was a youth, Mohammed Bokhari, and he and two accomplices were arrested and tortured by the Shah's secret police, SAVAK, during the course of which they implicated General Teymour Bakhtiar, a former head of SAVAK who had been dismissed and exiled by the Shah. All three conspirators were executed.

Two months later the so-called Marble Palace Plot culminated in another attempt on the Shah's life. As he arrived at his office on the morning of 10 April 1965, a man opened fire with a sub-machine-gun, killing two bodyguards and getting killed himself in the process. The Shah was unhurt. The would-be assassin was a young soldier, named Abadi. Twelve others were charged with conspiring against the Shah and served long terms of imprisonment. Bakhtiar's name was linked with this plot, and with two subsequent attempts, one of them during the Shah's visit to Berlin in 1967. In 1970 Bakhtiar was killed in Iraq, allegedly in a hunting accident.

Back in the United States, meanwhile, in February 1966, the civil rights leader and Black Muslim minister Malcolm X got up to make a speech at the Audubon Ballroom in New York City. Hardly had he begun when at least three men – the numbers involved are uncertain – walked towards the stage on which Malcolm X was standing alone and shot him dead. It was a well-organised attack. Two other men had started an argument in the audience, seconds before it happened, and a smoke-bomb had been let off, all to create a diversion and distract bodyguards and police. One assailant, Talmadge Hayer, was wounded and arrested, but the others escaped. Working on the theory that Malcolm X was murdered by co-religionists after a split in the movement, for he had formerly been second-in-command and heir-apparent to the Black Muslim movement's leader, the Honourable Elijah Muhammed, police arrested two men named Butler and Johnson, and they were convicted of the crime, along with Hayer. But doubts remain over this assassination. Malcom X had been waging a strong campaign against the victimisation of poor blacks in Harlem by drug-trafficking, gambling and prostitution, and there are grounds for suspecting that his death was arranged by the local Mob bosses who profited from these activities.

An African assassination in January 1966, that of the Prime Minister of Nigeria, Tafawa Balewa, was a *tribal* prelude to what seemed a much more significant *racial* assassination in South Africa on 6 September of that year. An earlier attempt on the life of Dr Verwoerd, the South African Prime Minister, in Johannesburg in 1960, following the Sharpeville massacre, had succeeded only in wounding him. A farmer, David Pratt, had walked up to the Prime Minister who was finishing a speech, and as Verwoerd turned towards him shot him twice in the face. This shooting was also seen by millions on TV. Pratt was declared mentally unbalanced and the Prime Minister recovered from his wounds.

Verwoerd was born in Holland and educated mainly in Germany before emigrating to South Africa. He was a fanatical racialist. During the 1930s he resigned a university professorship over the admission of European Jewish refugees into South Africa. He opposed South Africa's participation in the Second World War and supported Hitler. Becoming Prime Minister in 1958, it was he who reinforced and extended the policy of *apartheid* begun by Dr Malan and Johannes Strijdom before him; he who took South Africa out of the Commonwealth; and his government which sentenced Nelson Mandela to life imprisonment. Yet he was not finally killed by a conspiracy of the subject people, nor by his white political opponents. A parliament messenger, one Dimitrio Tsafendas, walked up to Dr Verwoerd in the parliament chamber and stabbed him several times in the neck and chest. The murderer was declared insane. He seems to have acted not because he was appalled by *apartheid* (though he was not technically white), but because he thought that if the government spent less on the blacks it could pay him higher wages.

Meanwhile, a neo-Nazi who had long been stirring up racial hatred in the United States was also killed for reasons not directly connected with his outrageous policies. George Lincoln Rockwell was leader of the National Socialist White People's Party and the author of *White Power*, whose hysterical message was that American whites must kill the 'damnable Jewish, Zionist, "nigger" and Communist enemy'. He once said: 'The only cure for Judaism is Dr Hitler's cure.' He had been committed to an institution for psychiatric observation in 1960. But he was consigned to physical as well as mental oblivion on 25 August 1967, by a sniper's bullet, in Arlington, Virginia. Fortunately, perhaps, his murderer turned out to be one of his own persuasion – John Patler, a former editor of the American Nazi Party's journal, *The Stormtrooper*, who had been expelled from the party after causing internal friction between dark and blond Nazis.

The same year saw an unsuccessful attempt in Haiti on the

life of the notorious 'Papa Doc' François Duvalier, whose brutally repressive family regime had been in operation for a decade and was to survive until 1986.

It was 1968 that shocked the world, as well as America, once again, however, when Dr Martin Luther King and Senator Robert F. Kennedy were murdered. It is possible to say that Dr King's death was both assassination and ritual sacrifice, even though there is no firm evidence that there was a conspiracy backing up his murderer, James Earl Ray. For a significant proportion of the white population of the southern states was itself a kind of conspiracy in its violent hatred of blacks. Dr King had received many death threats in his time and had been stabbed ten years earlier in New York. Police had threatened him in Nashville, Tennessee. Racial hatred was espoused by members of the Ku Klux Klan, the American Nazi party and other extreme white groups, and Martin Luther King, an educated and influential Negro and winner of the Nobel Peace Prize, was murdered as the foremost representative of black people's aspirations in the United States, and the most eloquent advocate of the racial equality that so many found – and still find – abhorrent.

James Earl Ray, who had a criminal record and a string of aliases, bought a rifle and a box of ammunition, booked into a cheap hotel in Memphis, Tennessee on 4 April 1968, and shot Dr King dead when he came on to the balcony of the Lorraine Motel across the street. Dr King had spoken prophetically of his own death in a speech the day before, saying, 'I'd like someone to mention that day that Martin Luther King tried to give his life serving others . . .'

Ray escaped to Canada, then to London, then to Portugal, eluding the FBI's manhunt for Dr King's murderer. Then a man posing as a Canadian named Sneyd was detained at London's Heathrow Airport and his fingerprints wired to Washington, where they were identified as those of James Earl Ray. He was extradited to the United States, where he pleaded guilty at his trial and was sentenced to imprisonment for life.

Much doubt has been thrown on the 'solitary killer' conclusion in Martin Luther King's case, as in so many other

American deaths by violence. Where did Ray get the money for all the travelling he did to elude arrest? How far did the FBI pursue its concern at the possibility of Luther's becoming a black 'Messiah' and the focus of a militant black nationalist movement? Hoover had ordered agents to tape-record King's extra-marital sexual encounters, transcripts of which were then offered to the press, but editors declined to use this material. There have been allegations that the underworld accomplices in Ray's escape were mobsters – possibly in league with the Ku Klux Klan – who paid Ray five thousand dollars to kill Dr King. Ray himself was a reputed smuggler of narcotics, and King had made powerful attacks on white organised crime which exploited poverty in the black urban ghettoes.

If there *was* a conspiracy behind Ray, it was a singularly ignorant one. It should have realised that the murder of the black leader would advance the cause of blacks rather than hold it back. The hatred remained, of course, and riots ensued across the United States, involving the deaths of more than 30 people, most of them blacks. A Ku Klux Klan 'Grand Dragon', speaking at a rally afterwards, said: 'You assassinate a king, a queen, the President of the United States, maybe even a governor, but who in the name of God ever heard of assassinating a nigger? I thought you killed them.' The man had a point, though not quite the one he thought he had. The implication of his remark is that the word assassination has something to do with dignity and importance. That is the danger I referred to in my introduction. It confers fame or infamy on its perpetrators, and provides scope for immature fantasies.

The man who killed Robert Kennedy shot him at point-blank range in the Ambassadors Hotel, Los Angeles, after a party, when the Senator was seeking the Democratic Party's Presidential nomination. Sirhan Bishara Sirhan, a Palestinian immigrant, was arrested, tried and sentenced to death for the crime, and was on Death Row in San Quentin awaiting execution when California abolished the death penalty. So Sirhan stayed in prison and is still there. Was he mentally deranged? Kennedy, a Catholic, seems to have died because Sirhan, an Arab, hated the Jews. He claimed that he went to the hotel on

5 June not knowing that Robert Kennedy was there, but that does not tie in with entries in his exercise-book diary to the effect that 'RFK must be disposed of'. The day was the first anniversary of the Six-Day War, and Sirhan held Kennedy responsible for American support for the Israelis against Palestinian interests.

There had been a number of threats against the Senator, however. The Teamsters union boss Jimmy Hoffa, for one, had made a threat against his life, and the people who perhaps profited most from Robert Kennedy's death were the Mafioso leaders of organised crime in America, upon whom both Kennedy brothers had declared war during JFK's presidency.

Argument has raged almost as fiercely over the conspiracy theory of Robert Kennedy's murder as over that of his brother. After his arrest, Sirhan vaguely mentioned Lyndon Johnson, Richard Nixon and Jimmy Hoffa in turn as having put him up to killing the Senator, and entries in his diary suggest that he associated the killing with cash payments. 'They can gas me,' he said after his arrest, 'but I am famous.' But did he really know what he was doing at all? The suggestion has been made that Sirhan was in a trance when he shot Kennedy, and Dr Bernard Diamond, a psychiatrist, found Sirhan an easily suggestible subject, inducing him at one point under hypnosis to climb the bars of his cell. Sirhan is known to have flirted with the occult, and has likened himself to the original *hassasin*, saying, 'It must have been something like that with me.'

Sirhan said in a television interview with David Frost, after twenty years in prison, that he sees nothing in his case which should prevent his release. He is not, after all, a mass murderer (he says), and he was not in full control of his senses at the time. The argument is hardly one to be taken seriously, of course, and the interesting question is whether he is in full control of his senses *now*.

A theory was spawned, apparently supported by some ballistic evidence but little else, that more than one person shot at Robert Kennedy in the Ambassadors Hotel that day. Persons present who testified that they *saw* Sirhan shoot Kennedy in the head have been asked to believe that Sirhan could not have fired the shots in question, because

138

post-mortem examination showed that the fatal shot was fired at point-blank range when all the witnesses testified to Sirhan's gun being two or three feet away from the Senator at the time. It was thought originally that eight shots were fired in all, three of which hit Kennedy, five of which wounded others. But subsequently suggestions were made that *more* than eight shots were fired, although Sirhan used an eight-chamber revolver; and that a hired security man who had links with organised crime shot Robert Kennedy whilst ostensibly returning Sirhan's fire.

It is perfectly obvious to most people outside the United States that a major part of the answer to the problem of reducing political violence there, as well as homicide of all types in that country, lies in the strict control of firearms. Rarely are the indications so clear. If we recall the murders and attempted murders of Presidents and aspiring Presidents alone, from the attempt on Andrew Jackson in 1835, followed by the murders of Lincoln, Garfield and McKinley and the attempts on the two Roosevelts and Truman, to the murders of the Kennedy brothers and the more recent attempt on Reagan, all ten of these murder bids have one common denominator – firearms. The framing of the law and its enforcement will not be easy, but this is the huge hurdle that the government of the United States must sooner or later tackle. An attempt to impose some federal controls was made by the Gun Control Act after the killing of Robert Kennedy, but restrictions were relaxed again in 1986 by Ronald Reagan, who permitted rifles and shotguns to be available once more on mail order.

The assassinations that saw out the shocking 1960s were not American but African, and to some extent, a sign of things to come – a Third World response to the examples set by the great powers and their allies. In February 1969, Eduardo Mondlane, a leader of Frelimo, the guerilla movement fighting for independence from Portugal, was blown up by a parcel bomb in Dar es Salaam. The bomb was alleged to have been sent to him by agents of the Portuguese government.

Tom Mboya was a Kenyan national leader and government minister after independence, noted for his moderation and seen as the natural successor of Jomo Kenyatta. But on the afternoon of 5 July 1969, the well-dressed young African Minister of Finance went shopping in Nairobi in his white Mercedes and was gunned down in the street as he left a shop, dying before he reached hospital. He was Africa's first post-colonial ministerial victim.

Mboya's killer was a Kikuyu, Nahashon Isaac Njenga Njoroge, who had been trained as an engineer in Bulgaria. At his trial he implicated the Kenya People's Union party, which was led by the communist Oginga Odinga. Njoroge had said to police at one point, 'Why pick on me? I only did as I was told. Why don't you go and get the big man?' But who the big man actually was, he resolutely refused to say during his trial. Njoroge was sentenced to death for the murder and hanged. It is not clear whether Mboya was killed by those who wished to prevent a fierce anti-communist from succeeding to power in Kenya, or by representatives of the poor who resented his success and his acceptance into the white man's world, or simply in an outbreak of tribal rivalry. But what happened as a result was that there were tribal riots, Mboya's Luo people angrily attacking the Kikuyu who had produced the killer of their hero, and the country was brought to the brink of civil war. Odinga was subsequently arrested and his party banned by Kenyatta for its allegiance to communist China.

In October, Dr Abdar-Rashid Ali Shermarke, the President of Somalia, was murdered in a left-wing military coup, and the African republics seemed all set to rival the Latin American record in bloody revolution.

11

Global Orgy

The 1970s opened with attempts on the lives of Pope Paul VI and Archbishop Makarios, President of the Cypriot republic. The pope narrowly escaped death in Manila during a visit to the Philippines in November 1970. Makarios escaped serious injury when his private helicopter was shot down in Nicosia by EOKA extremists. But it was 1971 that saw the first significant assassination of the decade, when the Prime Minister of Jordan and King Hussein's right-hand man, Wasfi-al-Tal, was shot dead on the steps of the Sheraton Hotel in Cairo by four members of the terrorist Black September movement.

In the United States, one Arthur Bremer made up his mind to shoot the President, Richard Nixon, in May 1972, but being frustrated by the strength of Nixon's security, he shot Governor George Wallace of Alabama instead, in Laurel, Maryland, wounding him severely. The immediate effect of this murder attempt was that Wallace, left half-paralysed, withdrew from the Presidential campaign and left the way open for Nixon, the man Bremer had intended to dispose of.

An attempt was made in the same year on the life of King Hassan II of Morocco by an air force attack on the royal palace. The king was one of the few monarchs still to rule by personal dictatorship at the time, and had many enemies both within and outside his own country.

On the island of Zanzibar off the coast of east Africa, Sheikh Abeid Karume had become President of the People's Republic after a communist coup in 1964, and he conducted a repressive and bloody dictatorship, even after Zanzibar had been linked with mainland Tanganyika in the new Commonwealth republic of Tanzania, under President Julius Nyerere. A small group of army officers, led by Lieutenant Hamud,

141

undertook to rid Zanzibar of this tyrant in 1972, and, while three soldiers held up Karume's guards, Hamud entered the room where Karume was playing cards with his comrades and opened fire with his machine-gun, killing Karume, but he was instantly shot dead himself by one of the dictator's bodyguards.

The African pattern of assassination continued with the murder by a Portuguese agent in June 1973 of Amilcar Cabral, leader of the revolutionary movement in Portuguese Guinea. Then, in 1976, Brigadier Murtala Ramal Mohamed, the Sandhurst-trained head of state in Nigeria, who had achieved a *coup d'état* in the previous year, was killed in another coup attempt which failed. And in 1977 the Congolese military leader who had assumed power in 1968 and became head of state, Marien N'Gouabi, was assassinated. Black Africans seemed to have become the world's newest political targets. But Bangladesh, too, suffered the usual crop of assassinations in an emerging nation. Sheik Mujibar Rahman, who had led Bangladesh to independence from Pakistan and become its Prime Minister, was massacred with his family in a military coup in August 1975, but then the new leader, Brigadier Khaled Mosharraf, was murdered in November.

Late in 1973, the Spanish Prime Minister, Carrero Blanco, was killed in Madrid by Basque terrorists. Admiral Luis Carrero Blanco, who was 70 years old, had been Franco's right-hand man for more than 30 years. The separatist movement ETA had planned to kidnap Blanco and hold him hostage until Basque prisoners were released from Franco's jails. But when Franco separated the roles of head of state and head of government, and appointed his loyal Catholic and anti-liberal colleague to the latter post, Blanco's security was stepped up, and the conspirators' plan, code-named Operation Ogro, was changed to assassination.

On 20 December, Blanco, after attending morning mass as usual, was on his way to his office in his armour-plated official car. Suddenly an explosion beneath the road blew the vehicle over 40 feet into the air, causing it to hit the parapet of a church. The bomb burst water mains and made a huge crater in the road. The Prime Minister's chauffeur and bodyguards were killed instantly, and Blanco was dead by the time he arrived at hospital. The killing was counter-productive, as far as the Basque extremists were concerned, because it brought Spain a step closer to the democracy which followed Franco's death and the succession of Juan Carlos as King of Spain, and did nothing for the separatist movement.

In 1975 attempts were made on the lives of King Faisal of Saudi Arabia and President Ford of the United States. Faisal's assailant was his nephew, Prince Faisal, who fired three shots at him in an attempt to avenge the death of his brother, Khalid, who had been shot dead by a police officer. Prince Faisal was incensed by the king's refusal to order the execution of Khalid's killer. The prince was himself executed instead by public beheading.

Gerald Ford was the target of two unrelated attacks by women within a month. The first assailant was a disciple of the mass murderer Charles Manson. The second, Sally Moore, was a former FBI informant who had been rejected, and who, with all the fury of a scorned woman, said, '. . . there comes a point when the only way you can make a statement is to pick up a gun.'

In March 1978, Aldo Moro, the Christian Democratic leader and former Prime Minister of Italy, was kidnapped and held hostage by Red Brigade terrorists attempting to obtain the release of thirteen fellow-anarchists in detention in Italian prisons. When the government refused to bargain with the kidnappers, they murdered the 62-year-old man who had been widely expected to become Italy's next President. His body was found in the boot of a car parked close to his party's headquarters in Rome. He had been shot eleven times. The kidnapping of Moro in a street of Rome in broad daylight had been a highly efficient operation, but, as is so often the case, the killing was counter-productive. It made a martyr of Moro, lost the Red Brigade many sympathisers, and failed to obtain the release of the prisoners whose freedom they sought.

The man who succeeded Pope Paul VI, when he died of a heart attack at the age of 81 in 1978, was Cardinal Albino Luciani, Patriarch of Venice, who assumed the name John Paul I. Within 33 days of his election, the new pontiff, 65 years old, was dead. He was found sitting up dead in bed, early in the morning of 29 September, with the light still on.

The officially announced cause of death was a heart attack, but there was no post mortem examination, and legitimate suspicions have arisen over the Vatican's reluctance to be entirely open on the matter. The pope had been assumed to be in excellent health, not least by the conclave which elected him. He had gone mountain climbing once a year when Patriarch of Venice, and had been pronounced fit in a thorough medical check-up before his election.

The author David Yallop came to the conclusion, after a three-year investigation of all the circumstances, that Pope John Paul I's sudden death was a case of assassination – the result of a conspiracy by shady financiers whose activities were about to be threatened by the pontiff's effort to cleanse the Vatican of financial corruption. The Italians are, as we have seen, past masters of assassination by poisoning, and the pope would have to have been poisoned, so that he died quietly during the night, rather than being murdered in public, an act which would clearly have resulted in an investigation which might lead – who knows where!

John Paul I had ordered an investigation into alleged fraud in the Vatican bank, and the day before his death announced that its head, Archbishop Marcinkus, was to be dismissed, along with other corrupt officials. Marcinkus was associated with the banker Roberto Calvi, financial adviser to the Vatican, who had links with the Italian Mafia, for which he laundered money, assisted by the Vatican bank. Calvi had been convicted of illegal financial dealings in Italy and had been sentenced to four years imprisonment and heavily fined. On paying the fine, he had been released pending his appeal against conviction. But in June 1982 he was found hanged under Blackfriars Bridge in London. The coroner's verdict was suicide, but a later inquest returned an open verdict. Pope John Paul II, meanwhile, had reversed, or at any rate suspended, his predecessor's attempt to drive the money-changers out of the temple.

The next victim to capture world headlines was Earl Mountbatten of Burma. In latter years Lord Mountbatten had taken an annual holiday with members of his family at Classiebawn Castle, a mansion on the coast of County Sligo in Ireland which had been built by Lord Palmerston and inherited by Edwina, Countess Mountbatten. Security advisers on both sides of the Irish Sea had thought it reasonably safe for him to continue going there, and in August 1979 Lord Mountbatten was enjoying himself at Classiebawn as usual. On the morning of the 27th, he went out fishing in his boat with his daughter and son-in-law, two grandsons, his son-in-law's mother, and a local Irish boy. A few minutes after leaving the harbour, the boat was blown up by a bomb which had been planted in it by the IRA. Lord Mountbatten, 79 years old, one of his grandsons and the local boy were killed. Eighty-three-year-old Lady Brabourne died from her injuries soon afterwards. The other grandson and his parents were seriously injured. This completely pointless terrorist attack was characteristic of the new climate of violent hatred which was consuming anti-democratic minorities throughout the world. It cannot even have been conceived as a possible means for achieving any political end.

Another victim of Irish terrorism, earlier in the same year, was Airey Neave, the Member of Parliament and close friend of Margaret Thatcher. The Irish National Liberation Army (INLA) planted a bomb under his car with a tilt device which caused it to explode as Mr Neave drove up the ramp from the House of Commons car park. A few days before this outrage, Sir Richard Sykes, the British ambassador to the Netherlands, had been murdered by members of the Red Brigade in an example of the increasing international cooperation among terrorists. The killing had been carried out, it was said, on behalf of the IRA.

North and South Korea had reached an agreement in 1972 by which they would attempt to co-exist in peace, but in 1979 the South Korean President, Park Chung Hee, was shot dead during a political rally, apparently in a North Korean attempt to destabilise the south. His wife had been killed in an earlier attempt on the President's life from which he escaped.

The 1980s opened with the murder of Archbishop Romero in El Salvador. Oscar Romero had been a fearless supporter of social reform and human rights, prominent among the Catholic clergy of Latin America. He was made Archbishop of San Salvador in 1977, and two years later was nominated for the

Nobel Peace Prize. But in March 1980, he was shot as he was celebrating mass at a hospital he had founded for terminally ill cancer patients. He spoke of the need to bring political violence to an end in that unhappy country, and, as he elevated the host, a man stepped forward and fired with a pistol at close range, piercing the archbishop's heart and lung. Witnesses said the gunman was accompanied by three others, but they were not identified. A right-wing para-military group was blamed for the killing.

In September, General Anastasio Somoza Debayle, the President of Nicaragua succeeding his murdered father and his elder brother, was assassinated in Paraguay, by the Sandinista Liberation Front, having fled from Nicaragua in the face of armed opposition to his notorious right-wing dictatorship.

Among the many victims of Middle Eastern conflict in 1981 were the President and Prime Minister of Iran, Muhammed Ali Rajai and Muhammed Bahonar. Rajai had won 89 per cent of the votes in the Presidential election in July of that year, but a bomb planted in the Prime Minister's office in Tehran at the end of August killed them both, as well as several others. Left-wing extremists were blamed for the bombing, and it was said that the man who planted the bomb was himself among those killed.

Many others were murdered in the crossfire of Iran's revolutionary and anti-revolutionary forces, and there were several plots against Ayatollah Khomeini, one of which, uncovered in 1982, resulted in the execution of nineteen men. The Ayatollah had an official taster to make sure that his food was not poisoned, and President Ali Rajai had once served in this capacity. The Shah had rejected a proposal to have Khomeini murdered in 1979, because it would have served the Ayatollah's ends rather than his own, but in 1982 Syrian intelligence revealed that President Hussein of Iraq, who had offered the Shah his support in 1979, was offering a reward of over £100 million to any professional killers who would dispose of Khomeini.

Bangladesh suffered another setback in May 1981 when President Zia Rahman, who had been in power for three years and was trying to restore democracy to that country after its period of emergency and instability in the seventies, was assassinated at Chittagong by rebel soldiers.

Also in 1981 the President of Egypt, Anwar Sadat, fell victim to Islamic fundamentalists. Sadat had signed a peace treaty with Prime Minister Begin of Israel, chiefly to save Egypt's floundering economy which had been crippled by military expenditure since the Six-Day War of 1967. For this initiative, he and Begin were jointly awarded the Nobel Peace Price for 1978, but all the Arab nations except Egypt were bitterly opposed to the treaty and regarded Sadat as a traitor to the Arab cause in general and in particular to the Palestinian fight for self-determination.

On 6 October 1981, Sadat was taking the salute at a military parade in a Cairo suburb when an army lorry drew up in front of him. Four soldiers jumped out as Sadat rose to his feet and opened fire with machine-guns, killing the President and several other officials. Some of the rebel soldiers were shot immediately, but others were brought to trial, revealing a huge conspiracy in the Egyptian army. In April 1982, President Mubarek rejected plans for clemency for five Muslim fundamentalists convicted of the assassination, and they were executed.

In that same year, attempts were made on the lives of President Reagan in Washington in March, Pope John Paul II in Rome in May, and Queen Elizabeth II in New Zealand in October. The shots fired at all three of them were *apparently* by isolated would-be murderers. John Hinkley, Reagan's assailant, shot the President in the chest, wounding three other people in the process. Reagan was out of hospital in less than a fortnight, surviving a serious shooting in the manner of the Wild West heroes he had once portrayed in Hollywood movies. Hinkley, who subsequently admitted that he was trying to impress the actress Jodie Foster (who had never heard of him), pleaded insanity and was committed to a mental institution before he faced trial, and this decision aroused much controversy. Five years later Hinkley was vainly campaigning for his freedom on the grounds that he was now sane!

The pope was shot whilst he was being driven in a jeep through St Peter's Square. The assailant was a militant Turkish terrorist, Mehmet Ali Agca. The pontiff, the Polish Karol Wojtyla, was seriously injured and underwent major intestinal surgery, after which he convalesced for six months. He subsequently presented the bullet which came close to killing him to the shrine of the Blessed Virgin Mary at Fatima in Portugal, whilst giving thanks for his delivery from assassination. His would-be murderer was sentenced to life imprisonment. After claiming at first that he had acted alone, Agca tried to blame the Bulgarian and Russian secret services for the affair, and three Bulgarians were accused but subsequently acquitted. The implication of Bulgaria apparently gained some credibility because of the moral support the Polish pope gives to Catholics in eastern Europe. Agca then said that he had been 'offered favours' to implicate the Bulgarians, and named Francesco Pazienza, who was associated with the Mafia. After three years of enquiry, the Italian authorities became convinced that Agca had been part of a conspiracy to end the pope's life. Two more attempts were to be planned against the pope, the first by a Spanish priest wielding a bayonet whilst John Paul was still convalescing after the first attack. Another potential assassin was a Turk, significantly enough for the copy-cat theory of assassination, who was arrested in Holland during the pope's visit there in 1985. Samet Aslan later committed suicide in prison.

The queen's assailant was a youth named Christopher Lewis, who fired a shot at her during the royal visit to Dunedin. He used a .22 rifle and the low-velocity bullet fell short of its target. Police and others who heard the report thought it was a car backfiring, and Lewis's plan was only revealed when he was arrested some weeks afterwards for an armed raid on a post office. He evidently had two accomplices, both schoolboys like himself. Committed to a mental institution, Lewis tried to escape in 1983, having formulated a plan to kill the Prince of Wales during *his* visit to New Zealand.

1982 saw the murder in Beirut of Lebanon's President-elect, Bachir Gemayel, who was killed by a bomb, and his murder provoked massacres in that volatile country.

The Philippines took the world stage in August 1983, with the assassination of the leader of the opposition, Benigno Aquino. He was shot at Manila airport as he descended the steps of an aircraft which had brought him back from exile in the United States. The government announced that a deranged airport worker, Rolando Galman, who had been shot dead, was responsible for the killing, but it is generally believed that the assassination was carried out at the instigation of the President, Ferdinand Marcos, and his wife Imelda. There had been several attempts on the lives of the Marcoses during their dictatorship. Imelda had been wounded in the arms and hands when defending herself against a would-be assassin armed with a knife. Aquino's widow Corazon subsequently became President, despite rigged elections, the United States having withdrawn its support from the corrupt Marcos and his oppressive dictatorship. Marcos died in exile in 1989, the murder of Aquino having achieved nothing but his own downfall.

Cory Aquino's Presidency of the Philippines has already survived several attempts to unseat her, and it is an inevitable by-product of the growing equality of women that they should be as exposed as men to assassination when they assume power over people's lives. Mrs Indira Gandhi was the first woman to exercise power over one of the world's largest populations, and as leader of India's ruling Congress Party she managed to steer a fairly triumphant, if increasingly autocratic, course through the difficult terrain of Indian politics, as well as maintaining her country's neutrality in international affairs.

Indira Gandhi was the daughter of Jawaharlal Nehru, the first Prime Minister of independent India, and her succession to her father's position, nearly two years after his death, established a family dynasty which is still going strong. Her husband, Feroze Gandhi, who was no relation to the Mahatma, had died of a heart attack in 1960. She became Prime Minister in 1966 and inaugurated a socialist programme which included the controversial promotion of birth control to limit the rising population of her country. She fell foul of her more reactionary opponents, and had many ups and downs, but worked genuinely for the welfare of her people and became an astute politician and a respected international figure.

It was her concern for Indian unity that led to her death. In 1984 members of a Sikh separatist movement took over and fortified the Golden Temple in Amritsar, the centre of the Sikh religion. The extremists were led by Sant Jarnail Singh Bhindranwale, who had been undermining the authority of the government for more than two years. Mrs Gandhi, long hesitant to move against Bhindranwale, finally felt forced to order the storming of the holy building by Indian troops with tanks, to remove the terrorists. In an operation called 'Blue Star', hundreds of innocent Sikhs were killed in the ensuing battle, as well as soldiers and terrorists. The operation was a major blunder, and Mrs Gandhi, never visualising such slaughter, was misled by her military advisers. All Sikhs were outraged by the invasion of their most sacred temple. Mrs Gandhi was advised to dismiss the Sikh members of her bodyguard as a precaution, but she refused, saying, 'I have nothing to fear from Sikhs.'

On the morning of the last day of October 1984, Indira Gandhi walked from her home towards a lawn where she was to be interviewed by Peter Ustinov, who was filming a documentary about her. Suddenly a Sikh member of her security guard, Beant Singh, stepped in front of her and fired three shots from a pistol into her abdomen. As she sank to the ground, another Sikh, Satwant Singh, opened fire with an automatic rifle. The Prime Minister was felled by 32 bullets. Her other bodyguards had dived for cover, and in the shock and confusion no one did anything for some seconds. The assassins made no attempt to escape, but stood there with their hands up. It was Mrs Gandhi's daughter-in-law Sonia who came running from the house and started giving orders, and the bleeding body was rushed to hospital, but the efforts of the surgeons failed to save Mrs Gandhi's life. The bullets had ruptured her liver and a lung, caused major damage to her intestines, shattered veins and arteries, and severed the spinal cord. 'Mrs Gandhi was probably dead by the time she hit the ground,' one surgeon said. She was 67.

A handwritten note found on Mrs Gandhi's desk said: 'If I die a violent death, as some fear and a few are plotting, I know the violence will be in the thought and action of the assassin, not in my dying – for no hate is dark enough to overshadow the extent of my love for my people and my country . . .'

The two Sikhs, belatedly arrested by police, were taken to a guardhouse. Within twenty minutes, shots were heard inside. Beant was shot dead, and Satwant seriously wounded. The official explanation was that they had made a violent escape bid. This seemed unlikely in view of their earlier behaviour, and the story was later denied by witnesses.

The murder was not intended to achieve anything. It was nothing more than a revenge killing, although wild theories began to circulate about conspiracies by Pakistan (which allegedly supported the Sikh separatists), or the CIA (because of Mrs Gandhi's ties with the Soviet Union). What the assassination did was to score an own goal, unleashing a campaign of vengeance by Hindus, and at least 2500 Sikhs were killed in the ensuing riots, many of them burned to death by rioters, watched by police and allegedly spurred on by Congress politicians. Men were hacked to death, women raped and boys castrated, and millions of pounds' worth of damage done to property, until Mrs Gandhi's son and immediate successor Rajiv – who was himself the subject of an assassination plot in the following year – belatedly brought the army in to restore order after three days.

In November 1986, General Arun Vaidya, the Indian Chief of Staff who had planned and led Operation 'Blue Star', was shot dead by four gunmen on motor-cycles. The surviving Sikh who shot Mrs Gandhi, Satwant Singh, and another bodyguard, Kehar Singh, with whom he and Beant had plotted the assassination, were finally hanged in Delhi on 6 January 1989.

Only a fortnight before Mrs Gandhi's murder, the IRA had attempted to assassinate the British Prime Minister and the entire Cabinet. The Irish terrorists were no more successful than the authors of the Gunpowder Plot or the Cato Street gang had been in their similar enterprises. Their bomb exploded on the sixth floor of the Grand Hotel at Brighton, where the Conservative Party was holding its annual conference, on the morning of 12 October 1984. Four people were killed and more than 30 wounded, some seriously, but it has to be said, even by one who does not admire her, that Margaret Thatcher's appearance, perfectly groomed as usual, only a few hours after the explosion, with the words 'It's business as usual', was a masterpiece of cool defiance, however she may have felt inside.

Patrick Magee, a former Norwich Cathedral altar boy turned IRA terrorist, was convicted of this bomb attack after being traced to a Glasgow tenement building eight months after the incident. He had planted the bomb behind panelling in the bathroom of Room 629, wrapped in clingfilm so as to disguise its distinctive smell from trained sniffer dogs. The bomb had been planted 24 days before it was timed to go off, early in the morning of the last day of the conference.

In a Supplement to the Report to the National Commission on the Causes and Prevention of Violence, published in the United States in 1970, explanations were offered for the practically non-existent history of assassination in Sweden. Some of the reasons put forward were that the kings had become willing figureheads rather than personal rulers; that there was no tradition of political violence; and that there had lately been close control over the use of firearms. But on the last day of February 1986, Sweden was shocked by the country's most sensational crime since the murder of King Gustavus in 1792. Olof Palme, the Swedish Prime Minister and United Nations mediator in the Iran-Iraq war, was shot dead in a Stockholm street. It is still not clear whether this was a case of murder by a deranged individual or political assassination, but the latter seems probable.

Olof Palme was the charismatic leader of the Social Democratic Party in Sweden, and was a radical and controversial figure, who had first come to international prominence when he had offered asylum in Sweden to young Americans who refused to serve in the Vietnam war. More recently he had founded the International Nuclear Disarmament Commission. On Friday, 28 February 1986, he and his wife Lisbeth went to a cinema in Stockholm with their son and his girlfriend. Palme had dimissed his bodyguards. When they left the cinema, Mr and Mrs Palme parted from the younger couple and were walking home when a man suddenly stepped out and fired two shots at Palme at point-blank range with a

Smith and Wesson revolver, then ran off into the night. There were other people about, and they heard the shots, but no one got a clear look at the killer, not even Lisbeth Palme. Her husband was rushed to hospital, but died there almost at once. He was 58.

The murderer had said nothing to Palme, and no individual or group has ever claimed responsibility for the killing – an unusual circumstance. Despite the detention of various suspects over the next few months, and the offer of a large reward for information leading to the solution of the mystery, Swedish police failed to identify the killer, and public criticism of the handling of the case mounted. Numerous resignations followed in both police and government offices.

After some time rumours of bribery and corruption in Sweden's high places began to be heard. A month before his death, Palme had been in India, visiting his friend the new Prime Minister, Rajiv Gandhi, and soon afterwards, a big arms contract was awarded by India to Sweden's ailing Bofors company in the face of strong competition from several other countries, including Britain, France and the United States. Palme was then posthumously awarded India's Nehru Prize for the promotion of peace and non-violence. There were allegations that Bofors had paid millions of pounds into Swiss bank accounts held by Indian politicians. More sinister still, it appeared that Palme had been doing arms deals with Iran even whilst he was on his peace mission in the Gulf on behalf of the United Nations. None of this has been proven, and it remains to be seen whether further investigation and revelations throw any light on Olof Palme's murder.

In apparent desperation for a scapegoat, one Christer Petterson was sentenced to life imprisonment for the murder, in July 1989, but in October the sentence was overturned by the appeal court, which concluded that the evidence produced to convict Petterson, based on identification by Palme's widow, was insufficient.

I had already begun to write, at this point, that the killing of Olof Palme was the last murder of a national leader to capture the world's headlines before I delivered this book to my publisher, but events have caught up with me. On 22 November 1989 – the 26th anniversary of the murder of John F. Kennedy – another nation's new President, René Moawad of Lebanon, was blown to bits by a car bomb in west Beirut. As far as this book is concerned, it brings the story full circle. The Middle East, it would seem, is the Alpha and Omega of assassination.

Moawad had been elected President only seventeen days before his death, during political and constitutional reforms backed by the Arab League and intended to bring peace to that troubled country, whose Prime Minister in 1987, Rashid Karami, had also been killed – by a helicopter explosion. President Moawad had attended celebrations of the 46th anniversary of Lebanon's independence from France. His car was in a motorcade passing a school when the remote-controlled bomb exploded. Twenty-two other people were killed, according to some reports, including Syrian and Lebanese soldiers, civilians, and five of the President's bodyguards. The 64-year-old President was decapitated in the blast, and his charred remains could only be identified by his wallet and jacket. It seemed likely that the large bomb was also intended to kill the Prime Minister, Dr Selim el-Hoss, and the Speaker, Mr Husseini, but they both escaped, travelling in separate cars behind the Presidential Mercedes.

René Moawad was a lawyer who had been a Member of Parliament since 1957, and he was a strong advocate of Muslim-Christian détente, intent on achieving permanent peace and stability in a land torn apart by fourteen years of civil war. 'Enough agony, enough blood, enough destruction,' he had said a few hours earlier on television. But his policies were bitterly opposed by Christian extremists led by General Michel Aoun, commander-in-chief of the Lebanese army, who called Moawad a Syrian puppet, and Aoun was immediately blamed for the murder by Syria. The assassination seems to bring a step closer the apparently inevitable partition of Lebanon.

Meanwhile, the murder of lesser-known and minor political figures goes on all the time. In one week (19–25 November 1989), a Basque separatist leader, Josu Muguruzu, was shot dead by masked gunmen in Madrid, and an opposition politi-cian was killed in India's general election. Most recently, in October 1990, the Speaker of the Egyptian parliament was shot dead, and Wolfgang Schaeuble, Germany's Interior Minister, was seriously wounded by two shots fired at him during a rally by one Dieter Kaufmann. Before this book appears in the shops, human aggression being what it is, another assassination of an internationally known politician will almost certainly have occurred.

12

The Extreme Form of Censorship

We have come a long way, in historical terms, since the assassinations of Ramses III, Sennacherib and Julius Caesar. Yet in the sense of political wisdom and morality we seem to have progressed hardly at all. Assassination has been employed regularly, since the beginnings of recorded history, and we have proved incapable of dispensing with it. Yet it has received practically no philosophical justification, except in the case of tyrannicide.

John of Salisbury and William of Occam, Machiavelli and John Knox, have given assassination their various blessings in different circumstances, and it has been defended in modern times on the grounds that the assassination of war-mongering kings and politicians is better than the loss of many thousands of innocent lives resulting from their evil policies. It is easy to make this assertion and then to pick out examples that support the argument. No one can seriously doubt that the killing of Caligula was in the best interests of the Roman people, or that the early death of Hitler, by whatever means, would have been a blessing to the modern world. But such outstanding and clear-cut cases cannot be multiplied indefinitely to produce a blanket excuse for political murder. The vast majority of assassinations have signally failed to benefit anybody, and a great many have produced results exactly the opposite of those hoped for. Cool and patient political judgement is not the most likely attribute of anyone whose temperament allows him to contemplate physical violence to achieve his ends.

'Assassination is the extreme form of censorship,' Bernard Shaw wrote. Censorship is a tool of intolerance resorted to in order to control human freedom, and we must condemn the self-appointed censor in political matters as rigorously as we do in literature and the arts.

In the course of this book there have been exhibited a great variety of reasons for the shedding of VIP blood by those, whether individuals or groups, who have felt themselves authorised to destroy life, not on the spur of the moment, as happens more often than not in cases of common murder, but after deliberate premeditation and careful planning. It appears to me that there are six categories of what are generally referred to as assassinations, into which all cases can fit more or less comfortably for purposes of analysis:

First, there are the cases of *tyrannicide*, in which a despotic personal ruler has been killed, ostensibly at least, for the sake of his suffering people. The murders of the Emperor Caligula, Tsar Alexander II and President Karume of Zanzibar can be cited as examples. But although the assassins' intentions *may* be honourable in such cases, their judgement of the consequences is not always sound. Alexander II, for instance, was succeeded by his second son, as Alexander III, who proved to be more of an oppressive tyrant than his father had been.

In other cases claimed as tyrannicide, there may not be universal agreement about whether the murdered ruler was a tyrant or not. The conspirators who killed Caesar accused him of tyranny, but were the Roman people unduly oppressed? Would they have voted in a referendum for his elimination? There is no room for consensus politics in the theory of tyrannicide, but it remains the one form of assassination against which, in particular cases, it is difficult to argue, either from a practical or a moral standpoint.

The second type is the *rival* assassination. This may be on behalf either of a personal ruler who feels his position to be under threat from a challenger, or of an aspiring ruler who believes his own claim to power justifies the displacement of his rival by violence if it cannot be achieved by other means. It is often an accompaniment – though rarely an entirely necessary one – of a revolution or a *coup d'état*. We may recall the cases of Trotsky and Benigno Aquino as instances of the first kind, and those of King Wenceslaus and Giuliano de' Medici as instances of the second. The classic family rivalry between the Karageorgeviks and the Obrenovics in nineteenth-century Serbia embraced both kinds of rival assassination.

Sometimes, the latter type of ruler, the usurper, is responsible for further rival assassination *after* he has achieved power, in order to prevent his deposed rival from reasserting himself, as was the case with Tsar Peter III and probably King Richard II. The murders of some of the medieval popes belong in this category, too, for however pious the characters involved may have seemed, and however paramount the arguments over religious doctrine, they were really cases of political rivalry.

The rival assassination was the type that Machiavelli was chiefly referring to in *The Prince*, based on his knowledge and experience of the Italian city states in the fifteenth and sixteenth centuries, and it was his view that a ruler 'must not worry if he incurs reproach for his cruelty so long as he keeps his subjects united and loyal. By making an example or two he will prove more compassionate than those who, being too compassionate, allow disorders which lead to murder and rapine. These nearly always harm the whole community, whereas executions ordered by a prince only affect individuals.'

Machiavelli was surely wrong in this belief. He took no account of the sensibilities of mass psychology, and failed to realise that the resort to violence is already an admission of defeat.

Nevertheless, it matters not who is the most virtuous and benevolent ruler in these cases – the overthrown or the triumphant. For that can only be seen after the event, and if there is to be any moral imperative in this category it must be that such killing is always wrong unless the murdered rival was a tyrant, in which case it belongs not to this category, but to the first.

The third type of political killing that has been widespread is the *expedient* assassination. This means the permanent removal of someone who is not necessarily the rival of a ruler or leader, but who is conceived as a dangerous enemy of the state, threatening to undermine its power and authority, or as a political nuisance – a thorn in the flesh or an embarrassment to the individual or group that desires his elimination. Examples of this category of victim include Thomas Becket, Don Carlos and Rasputin. The ritual sacrifice of kings would also come into this category.

This is where – in the modern world at least – the shadowy backcloth of secret and intelligence services come into dim view most often, the public at large being kept mainly in the dark, lacking enough information to enable it to form intelligent judgements of right or wrong in the matter until long after the event. But there are undoubtedly many instances of this type of assassination for which strong arguments could be made in the political climate of the time. Assassinations of powerful enemy figures in wartime all come into this category, and the undercover promotion by leading Spaniards of William the Silent's assassination, for instance, even though it backfired when finally successful, seemed to make good sense to the Spanish, though it was a tragedy for the Dutch and their allies.

The fourth kind is the *terrorist* assassination. This is employed by minority groups for propaganda purposes and in attempts to intimidate those holding power and force their own political ends on the majority. Instances of this type of killing are those of Count Bernadotte and Aldo Moro.

There is, of course, no possible reasonable defence of this anti-democratic activity in the modern world. If revolutionaries achieve power by violence and terror, why should anyone believe for a moment that they will not use the same violence and terror in maintaining their power and enforcing their will on everyone else? This is what usually happens when violent revolution succeeds – one repressive regime is replaced by another.

The fifth category is what we might call *symbolic* assassination. It is carried out not with the hope of achieving political change, but as an end in itself – the elimination of a representative figure in a hated order or system. Sometimes it is an act of revenge – a retaliation against a conceived injustice or political disaster. The killing of Marat, the Archduke Franz Ferdinand and Indira Gandhi can be taken as examples. The assassins in such cases are often so blinded by

159

overpowering hatred that they do not even make any pretence of having thought about the consequences of their actions.

The sixth and last type of so-called assassination is the act committed by isolated lunatics, who may or may not be deluded into thinking they are acting in the interests of others. If we have to give it a name other than murder we can call it the *paranoid* assassination. It is usually the product of a mind consumed with a sense either of personal grievance against the victim, or of self-exaltation in the delusion that the killer has a divine mission to commit the act. Instances of this kind are the murders of Spencer Perceval and James Garfield.

Sometimes there is considerable overlapping between these six types of assassination, and it is difficult to decide whether a certain case qualifies for one group or another. But I believe that all assassinations and attempted assassinations can be accommodated within these six categories.

I now come back, however, to the argument of my introduction – that most so-called assassinations are really nothing more than murders in public, and should not be accorded the dignity of extraordinary titles. In the six categories I have distinguished, only those falling into the first can have any real defence or justification in the thinking of reasonable human beings, as altruistic acts committed for the advantage of the people as a whole, and not in the narrow interests of those who decided to act.

Even those cases have often been ill-judged or misguided. The well-meaning conspirators who have disposed of a tyrant have not always thought the political consequences through sufficiently to be certain that the victim would not be replaced by another tyrant as bad or even worse, and their action has thus turned out in practice, if not in theory, to be *against* the interests of the people.

As the vast majority of assassinations fall not into the category of tyrannicide, but into the other five, it is immediately obvious that assassination can only very rarely be regarded, with hindsight, as an act meriting any praise, and it is because of this extreme scarcity of demonstrable profit that it has received such scant regard among political thinkers.

That being so, it surely follows that if the killings in the other five categories, which include by far the largest number, are generally to be condemned, there is no logical reason to call them by a name which imparts a kind of distinction on deeds which are no more commendable than those of a common criminal, and indeed elevates the killer into a kind of hero in the public mind. All such acts should be referred to as *murder*, so that the word *assassination*, if it is to be a necessary part of our vocabulary at all, can be reserved for those rare cases in history which are judged to be the destruction of human life by a consensus of honourable or well-intentioned men for the benefit of society as a whole and not out of self-interest or delusion. And for these there is already a sufficient title – tyrannicide.

Perhaps then the idea of assassination will lose that dangerous aura of sensationalism which can attract people, imparting to the would-be assassin not the image of a dishonourable and unbalanced murderer but a courageous and romantic rebel. The sinister and lasting appeal of assassination is evident in the rumours surrounding the deaths of such as Alexander the Great, Napoleon and Stalin, among others, reinforced, perhaps, by a confusion of the possession of power with physical health and strength, so that the natural death of a ruler or person at the apparent height of his power always excites suspicion and breeds speculation. Even in England, alleged abhorrence of assassination notwithstanding, the taste for suspicion and intrigue lingers on. Nothing illustrates it more graphically than Macaulay's own passage on the death of Charles II (from a stroke) in 1685:

At that time the common people throughout Europe, and nowhere more than in England, were in the habit of attributing the deaths of princes, especially when the prince was popular and the death unexpected, to the foulest and darkest kind of assassination. Thus James the First had been accused of poisoning Prince Henry. Thus Charles the First had been accused of poisoning James the First. Thus when, in the time of the Commonwealth, the Princess Elizabeth died at Carisbrooke, it was loudly asserted that Cromwell had

161

stooped to the senseless and dastardly wickedness of mixing noxious drugs with the food of a young girl whom he had no conceivable motive to injure. A few years later, the rapid decomposition of Cromwell's own corpse was ascribed by many to a deadly potion administered in his medicine. The death of Charles the Second could scarcely fail to occasion similar rumours. The public ear had been repeatedly abused by stories of Popish plots against his life. There was, therefore, in many minds, a strong predisposition to suspicion; and there were some unlucky circumstances which, to minds so predisposed, might seem to indicate that a crime had been perpetrated. The fourteen Doctors who deliberated on the King's case contradicted each other and themselves. Some of them thought that his fit was epileptic, and that he should be suffered to have his doze out. The majority pronounced him apoplectic, and tortured him during some hours like an Indian at a stake. Then it was determined to call his complaint a fever, and to administer doses of bark. One physician, however, protested against this course, and assured the Queen that his brethren would kill the King among them. Nothing better than dissension and vacillation could be expected from such a multitude of advisers. But many of the vulgar not unnaturally concluded, from the perplexity of the great masters of the healing art, that the malady had some extraordinary origin. There is reason to believe that a horrible suspicion did actually cross the mind of Short, who, though skilful in his profession, seems to have been a nervous and fanciful man, and whose perceptions were probably confused by dread of the odious imputations to which he, as a Roman Catholic, was peculiarly exposed. We cannot, therefore, wonder that wild stories without number were repeated and believed by the common people. His Majesty's tongue had swelled to the size of a neat's tongue. A cake of deleterious powder had been found in his brain. There were blue spots on his breast. There were black spots on his shoulder. Something had been put into his snuffbox. Something had been put into his broth. Something had been put into his favourite dish of eggs and ambergrease. The Duchess of Portsmouth had poisoned him in a cup of chocolate. The Queen had poisoned him in a jar of dried pears. Such tales ought to be preserved; for they furnish us with a measure of the intelligence and virtue of the generation which eagerly devoured them.

I might add that the popular readiness to believe the worst has in no way diminished. In our own time, the deaths of Marilyn Monroe, Hugh Gaitskell and Rudolf Hess, to mention but three, have been subjects of widespread speculation. As far as I am aware, no one has yet come up with an elaborate theory to the effect that the deaths of three Russian leaders in rapid succession in the early eighties – Brezhnev, Andropov and Chernenko – were engineered by supporters of Mikhail Gorbachev's bid for power, but that is because he is seen on Russia's and the world's credit side. I, for one, hope he remains so, but such is human nature that, if he should fall from grace, someone is sure to remember that Gromyko once said of him, 'This man has a nice smile, but he has got iron teeth,' and start looking for the bite marks.

We have noted the gradual diminution of regicide, from the times of the ancient kings and Roman emperors to the last surviving absolute monarchs, and of tyrannicide, as the peoples of the world have struggled towards constitutional government and democracy. So how can we account for the fact that the last few decades – say from the end of the Second World War – have seen an apparent crescendo in political killing, which is continuing, and belies Edward Hyams' claim that the period at the end of the nineteenth century and up to the First World War was the 'golden age' of assassination? That was a period when anarchy was on the rampage in Europe. We now have a world-wide epidemic of murder in public.

Yet there are significant patterns in its occurrence. If the influence of climate upon assassination were to be studied, statistical observers would doubtless find that there seem to be some parts of the world which are prone to assassination as others might be to earthquake or volcanic eruption. In short, Russia notwithstanding, assassination flourishes in hot climates.

163

The temperament of peoples and nations is inevitably influenced by their environments, and it is not especially surprising that volatile politics and internal instability, producing assassinations with some frequency, coincide with high murder rates. In northern Europe, countries such as Britain, Denmark, Sweden and the Netherlands, which have high suicide but low murder rates, also have the lowest incidence of assassination. It is clearly a case of the extrovert versus the introvert temperament.

The violence of the twentieth century seems to lend support to the conviction, derived partly from Darwin, that man is an innately aggressive animal. The 'survival of the fittest' in politics goes hand in hand with the Machiavellian view that the end justifies the means. But the struggle of humanity towards civilisation, and the relative contentment with, or at any rate resignation to, the democratic process which has been achieved in much of Europe, is *hampered* by assassination rather than being advanced by it.

The human weakness for wanting to bring the man of power off his ill-deserved pedestal derives from the primeval view of the limitations and responsibilities of tribal kingship, and is on the whole a sensible suspicion of the arrogance of power. Lone assassins are moved to kill kings, as mountaineers seek to reach the highest peaks, because they are there, and it is arguable that when mankind has at last become sufficiently mature to dispense with kings and emperors, pharaohs and fuehrers, khans and tsars, shahs and sultans, popes and ayatollahs, then the temptations of assassination will fade from men's minds. But in the modern world, the aggressive and hot-headed response to despised authority goes overboard from opposition into hatred. The savagery of so many assassinations betrays an unhealthy hatred which is a stronger incentive than any ostensibly political justification for the murders.

There is little logic behind most so-called assassinations, and assassins motivated by hatred of their victims, rather than by logical consideration of the consequences, lack the political maturity to lead their people, who are the supposed beneficiaries of their actions, towards peace and democracy. They are therefore the enemies of wholesome human society.

Their immaturity is often betrayed by the very names the conspiratorial groups like to give themselves, like secret societies or gangs in boys' comics – Black Hand, Black Dragon, Red Brigade, Black September, and so on. They have not learned the lessons of history; in particular, the dangers of assassination shown up by many of the instances we have noticed, and which I have called the three Laws of Assassination:

1. The murder of a national leader loved and respected by the *majority* will always have the opposite effect to that intended. It reinforces the will of the majority to resist change brought about by violent means.

2. Murder inspired by hatred of an individual in a strong position of authority confuses the man with the policy, and may well lead to stern reinforcement of the policies by an even more zealous successor. No individual is indispensable to a strong system.

3. The killing of a person who is himself an extremist, leading or supporting a powerfully repressive regime, will very likely be followed by savage reprisals against the innocent as well as the guilty.

Machiavelli was well aware of the dangers facing those who wished to unseat his prince:

One of the most powerful safeguards a prince can have against conspiracies is to avoid being hated by the populace. This is because the conspirator always thinks that by killing the prince he will satisfy the people; but if he thinks that he will outrage the people, he will never have the courage to go ahead with his enterprise, because there are countless obstacles in the path of a conspirator. As experience shows, there have been many conspiracies but few of them have achieved their end. This is because the conspirator needs others to help him, and those have to be men who, he believes, are disgruntled. But as soon as he reveals his mind to a man who is dissatisfied he gives him the means to get satisfaction, because by telling all he knows the latter can hope to obtain all he wants. Seeing the sure profit to be won by

informing, and the highly dangerous and doubtful alternative, a man must be either a rare friend indeed or else
an utterly relentless enemy of the prince to keep faith
with you. To put it briefly, I say that on the side of the
conspirator there is nothing except fear, envy, and the
terrifying prospect of punishment; on the side of the
prince there is the majesty of government, there are
laws, the resources of his friends and of the state to
protect him. Add to all these the goodwill of the people,
and it is unthinkable that anyone should be so rash as to
conspire. For whereas in the normal course of events a
conspirator has cause to fear before he acts, in this case
he has cause for fear afterwards as well, seeing that the
people are hostile to him. He will have accomplished this
crime, and, because the people are against him, he will
have no place of refuge.

Alas, Machiavelli's modern disciples, inspired all too often by
personal hatred rather than political judgement, have not
bothered to read his intelligent message of caution.

Because assassination cannot, by any stretch of the imagination, be shown to have been beneficial in the modern world,
except in a small number of isolated instances of tyrannicide,
it does not have a respectable image. The world progresses
slowly towards attainment of humanity's ideals without
assassination, and murder inspired by frustration and impa-
tience, so far from hastening the process, often arrests it.

It is a necessary step on the way to peace, freedom, internal
harmony and the international cooperation the world so
badly needs, that killing should be removed from the agenda
of political options. When governments have finally rejected
killing, whether it be by war, by the sort of savage repression
seen recently in China and eastern Europe, and by capital
punishment, it will be an important step on the way to eliminating assassination, too. Politics as a blood sport is unprofitable, not merely because of any religious dogma about the
sacredness of human life but because common sense shows
that when life is held cheap the effect on societies is pervasive
and malignant.

Select Bibliography

This is in no sense a comprehensive bibliography of the vast subject of assassination. It merely lists those published works on which I have chiefly relied, and to which interested readers might choose to turn for more detailed information on specific cases. For some of the more up-to-date assassinations I have also relied on newspaper and television news reports.

Barlow, Frank *William Rufus*, Methuen, 1983
———— *Thomas Becket*, Weidenfeld & Nicolson, 1986
Barnes, John *Eva Peron*, W. H. Allen, 1978
Bernier, Olivier *Louis the Beloved*, Weidenfeld & Nicolson, 1984
Brook-Shepherd, Gordon *Victims of Sarajevo*, Harvill Press, 1984
Bruce, Marie Louise *The Usurper King*, Rubicon Press. n.d.
Bullock, Alan *Hitler: A Study in Tyranny*, Odhams Press, 1952
Burman, Edward *The Inquisition*, Aquarian Press, 1984
Chamberlain, E. R. *The Fall of the House of Borgia*, Temple, Smith, 1974
Cooke, Alistair *Talk About America*, Bodley Head, 1968
Cottrell, John *Anatomy of an Assassination*, Muller, 1966
Crankshaw, Edward *The Fall of the House of Habsburg*, Longmans, 1963
Crotty (Ed.), Wm. J. *Assassination and the Political Order*, Harper & Row, 1972
Davies, A. J. & A. B. *The Assassination of Julius Caesar*, F. Watts, 1975
Ehrenpreis, Irvin *Swift: The Man, His Works, and the Age*, Methuen (3 vols), 1962–83

Erickson, Carolly *Bloody Mary*, Dent, 1978

Ettinger, Elzbieta *Rosa Luxemburg: A Life*, Pandora Press, 1988

Fox, Robin Lane *Alexander the Great*, Allen Lane, 1973

Frank, Gerold *An American Death*, Hamish Hamilton, 1972

Fraser, Antonia *Mary Queen of Scots*, Weidenfeld & Nicolson, 1969

———— *Cromwell, Our Chief of Men*, Weidenfeld & Nicolson 1973

Frazer, Sir James *The Golden Bough*, Macmillan, 1957 edn.

Freeman, Ruth *Death of a Statesman*, Robert Hale, 1989

Freud, Sigmund *Totem and Taboo*, Routledge & Kegan Paul, 1950 edn.

Garmonsway, G. N. (tr.) *The Anglo-Saxon Chronicle*, Everyman's Lib. edn., 1953

Gerachty, Tony *The Bullet-Catchers*, Grafton Books, 1988

Gibbon, Edward *Decline and Fall of the Roman Empire*, Everyman's Lib. edn. (6 vols.), 1954

Gillen, Mollie *Assassination of the Prime Minister*, Sidgwick & Jackson, 1972

Goldschmidt, Arthur *A Concise History of the Middle East*, Westview Press, 1988 edn.

Graham, Robert *Spain: Change of a Nation*, Michael Joseph, 1984

Grant, Michael *The Roman Emperors*, Weidenfeld & Nicolson, 1985

Graves, Robert and Joshua Podro *The Nazarene Gospel Restored*, Cassell, 1953

Griffiths, Arthur *Chronicles of Newgate*, Chapman & Hall, 1884

Gupte, Pranay *India: The Challenge of Change*, Mandarin, 1989

Hart, B. H. Liddell *History of the Second World War*, Cassell, 1970

Hibbert, Christopher *The Rise and Fall of the House of Medici*, Allen Lane, 1974

———— *The French Revolution*, Allen Lane, 1980

Hingley, Ronald *Joseph Stalin: Man and Legend*, Hutchinson, 1974

Huizinga, J. *Erasmus of Rotterdam*, Phaidon Press edn., 1952

Huxley, Aldous *Grey Eminence*, Chatto & Windus, 1941

Hyams, Edward *Killing No Murder*, Nelson, 1969

Ivanov, Miroslav *The Assassination of Heydrich*, Hart-Davis, McGibbon, 1973

James, E. O. *The Ancient Gods*, Weidenfeld & Nicolson, 1960

Johnson, Paul *A History of the Modern World*, Weidenfeld & Nicolson, 1983

Kee, Robert *The Green Flag*, Weidenfeld & Nicolson, 1972

Kelly, J. N. D. *The Oxford Dictionary of Popes*, Oxford Univ. Press, 1986

Kirkham, James F. et al (eds). *Assassination and Political Violence*, Praeger, 1970

Laing, Margaret *The Shah*, Sidgwick & Jackson, 1977

Lane, Mark *Rush to Judgment*, Bodley Head, 1966

Longford, Elizabeth *Victoria R.I.*, Weidenfeld & Nicolson, 1964

Macalpine, Ida and Richard Hunter *George III and the Mad Business*, Allen Lane, 1969

Macaulay, Lord *A History of England*, (London) 1848–55

MacDonald, Callum *The Killing of SS Obergruppenführer Reinhard Heydrich*, Macmillan, 1989

Machiavelli *The Prince*, Penguin edn., 1961

Maclear, Michael *Vietnam: The Ten Thousand Day War*, Eyre Methuen, 1981

McConnell, Brian *Assassination*, Leslie Frewin, 1969

McNeal, Robert H. *Stalin: Man and Ruler*, Macmillan, 1988

Manchester, William *The Death of a President*, Michael Joseph, 1967

Mazour, Anatole *Russia: Tsarist and Communist*, Van Nostrand, 1962

Moorehead, Caroline *Fortune's Hostages*, Hamish Hamilton, 1980

Mosley, Nicholas *The Assassination of Trotsky*, Michael Joseph, 1972

Motley, John L. *The Rise of the Dutch Republic*, Warne edn. (3 vols.) n.d.

Mousnier, Roland *The Assassination of Henry IV*, Faber, 1973

Murray, Margaret A. *The Splendour that Was Egypt*, Sidgwick & Jackson, 1964 edn.

Palmer, Alan *The Life and Times of George IV*, Weidenfeld & Nicolson, 1972

Plume, Christian and Pierre Demaret *Target: De Gaulle*, Secker & Warburg, 1974

Plutarch *The Rise and Fall of Athens: Nine Greek Lives*, Penguin edn., 1960

————— *Makers of Rome: Nine Lives*, Penguin edn., 1965

Proyer, Ronald *Famous Stories of Assassination*, Arthur Barker, 1973

Ranelagh, John *The Agency: The Rise and Decline of the CIA*, Weidenfeld & Nicolson, 1986

Ridley, Jasper *Napoleon III and Eugenie*, Constable, 1979

Royle, Trevor *The Kitchener Enigma*, Michael Joseph, 1985

Russell of Liverpool, Lord *The Scourge of the Swastika*, Cassell, 1954

Scheim, David E. *The Mafia Killed President Kennedy*, W. H. Allen, 1988

Scott, Peter Dale et al (eds.) *The Assassinations*, Random House, 1976

Seward, Desmond *The First Bourbon: Henry IV of France & Navarre*, Constable, 1971

Shirer, William L. *The Rise and Fall of the Third Reich*, Secker & Warburg, 1960

Simmons, Ernest J. *Tolstoy*, Routledge & Kegan Paul, 1973

Smith, Lacey Baldwin *Treason in Tudor England*, Cape, 1986

Smith, Denis Mack *Mussolini*, Weidenfeld & Nicolson, 1981

Smith, Sir Sydney *Mostly Murder*, Harrap, 1959

Sparrow, Gerald *The Great Assassins*, John Long, 1968

Stenton, F. M. *Anglo-Saxon England*, Oxford Univ. Press, 1943

Suetonius *The Twelve Caesars*, Penguin edn., 1957

Swift, Jonathan *Gulliver's Travels*, Everyman's Lib. edn., 1940

Szulc, Tad *Fidel: A Critical Portrait*, Hutchinson, 1987

Taheri, Amir *The Spirit of Allah*, Hutchinson, 1985

————— *Holy Terror*, Hutchinson, 1987

Wedgwood, C. V. *William the Silent*, Jonathan Cape, 1944

Wilson, Colin *Order of Assassins*, Hart-Davis, 1972

SELECT BIBLIOGRAPHY

Wright, Peter *Spycatcher*, Heinemann, 1987
Yallop, David *In God's Name*, Jonathan Cape, 1984
Ziegler, Philip *Mountbatten*, Collins, 1985

Index

INDEX

THE ASSASSINATION FILE

174

INDEX

INDEX

INDEX